MADE ALIVE
IN CHRIST

Sermons from Paul's Letter
to the Ephesians

Graeme Stockdale

CONTENTS

INTRODUCTION

It is now forty years since I was ordained as a Baptist Minister, having spent the earlier years of my working life as an industrial chemist, initially employed by what was then the National Coal Board, and subsequently working in power stations and in a regional coal analysis laboratory for the Central Electricity Generating Board.

After training at an Anglican college (St John's Theological College, Nottingham) to be a Baptist minister – yes! That is not a misprint! – I served in three Baptist churches, in Leicester, Weston-super-Mare and Kettering, before retiring to a former mining village in Derbyshire.

In my 12 years of retirement I can honestly say I have had few days of boredom, apart from a period following hospitalisation, having succumbed to Covid-19. I occupy myself with what I term "controlled busyness" and am not one of these retired ministers who bemoans the fact that he is busier now than before retirement. I believe it is all a matter of choice, and I choose to spend my time in all aspects of gardening, with some study of various disciplines thrown in on rainy days, some time spent playing computer games, and in other activities.

I still preach in a few Baptist churches, limiting myself nowadays to just one engagement a month. This is a far cry from the pre-retirement treadmill of twice every Sunday! That "pre-retirement treadmill", however, means I have collected a substantial body of sermons over my forty years of preaching.

This had led me to spend another part of my time converting sermon notes into sentences, editing sermons and uploading them to Amazon Kindle as a way of storing the sermons in a readable form, and making them available to anyone who might find them useful. Through Kindle I have also been able to publish the books as paperbacks, and even hardback books.

So far I have published more than a dozen books, usually making them available free of cost from time to time. I have also developed the habit of taking copies to churches where I preach in order to make them available, free of charge, to anyone interested. In this way I hope that God's Word continues to be spread in increasing circles.

This book contains a selection of sermons from the Letter to the Ephesians. Although I refer to it as a "selection", unlike my other books, it does cover all chapters, including the dreaded "Wives submit…" passage!

Just a brief comment about the style of writing. Please bear in mind that these sermons were originally the spoken word, and therefore rules of grammar and style will have been broken! I have retained some of this style, which may occasionally create difficulty for the reader. Maybe it would be worth trying to "hear" the words in your head.

I have enjoyed going through these sermons again and am grateful for the way I believe God has inspired me through the years. I hope that readers will also find the sermons helpful to the praise and glory of our wonderful God.

Graeme Stockdale
January 2024

An 8th century prayer:-

Eternal Light, shine in our hearts;
Eternal Goodness, deliver us from evil;
Eternal Power, be our support;
Eternal Wisdom, scatter the
darkness of our ignorance;
so that with all our hearts and mind
and strength we may seek your face,
and be brought by your infinite
mercy to your holy presence;
Through Jesus Christ our Lord. AMEN

EPHESIANS 1:7

Ephesus was a great city. In fact, it was ranked as one of the greatest cities in the ancient world, and was certainly the most important city in Asia Minor. Pergamum was the regional capital but Ephesus surpassed Pergamum in every respect.

Ephesus had a harbour, which was prone to silting up, but which, when kept clear, provided an important trade route down the river to the Aegean Sea. In the opposite direction, Ephesus was the gateway to the rest of the region.

This great city stood at the intersection of several major trade routes - north, south, east and west - and so was an important centre of commerce.

There was a huge temple there, dedicated to the goddess Diana, or Artemis, as she was also known in the Greek speaking world. This temple was one of the seven great wonders of the ancient world, along with the hanging gardens of Babylon and the Great Pyramid. Ephesus was therefor an important religious centre.

There were also other temples, including temples

dedicated to the Roman emperors, Claudius and Nero, making Ephesus also a place of political importance within the Roman empire.

Unfortunately Ephesus was a notoriously evil place, attracting criminals and other disreputable people.

And for the apostle Paul, Ephesus was a centre for evangelism. He made it his base for the best part of three years. Paul stayed longer in Ephesus than anywhere else, as far as we know, and he formed a very close bond with the people there, as is shown by his moving farewell speech in Acts 20.

William Barclay writes: *"a more unpromising soil for sowing the seed of Christianity can scarcely be imagined, and yet it was there (in Ephesus) that Christianity had some of its greatest triumphs".*

The church in Ephesus is associated with Timothy, he being its first bishop, and also with Aquila and Priscilla and Apollos, and even the apostle John. It had a great history and important people held key positions in the church.

So, Ephesus was a great church, and by worldly standards, a great city, but it was not an easy place to live if you were a Christian, with all the conflicting lifestyles and messages making it a real struggle for believers to stay focussed on the gospel, the way of truth, the way of Christ.

So Paul writes to the believers in the church at

Ephesus, writing to remind them of the things that really matter above all else. Not the transient things of this world but the eternal and lasting things of God.

For centuries philosophers have wrestled with questions such as: *what is the meaning of life? what's it all about? what are we here for? what's the purpose behind it all?*

These are some of life's great questions that have exercised people's thinking from the very beginning of human history, and Paul offers an answer here. He tells us what it's all about - God's purpose for men and women. Here it is... Eph 1:v4 ***God chose us in him (Jesus Christ) before the creation of the world to be <u>holy</u> and <u>blameless</u> in his sight.***

Why? - v 5 ***In love he predestined us <u>to be adopted as his sons through Jesus Christ, in accordance with his pleasure and will.</u>***

This is God's purpose for us. This is what we are here for. To become children of God, knowing God not simply as some impersonal life force, or the source of cosmic energy, or even as the great, all-powerful Creator of all things. God's purpose is that everyone should know him - the God and Father of our Lord Jesus Christ - as *our* God and *our* Father.

Back in the first chapter of Genesis we are told that we are created in the ***image of God.*** What does this mean? It means, among other things, that we are created for a relationship with God, we are given the capacity for fellowship with God, we are created with potential to be holy, as God is holy, to be blameless children of God.

Indeed, it's this that distinguishes us from animal life, placing humans above the rest of the animal kingdom.

Humans are created in the image of God; the human race was intended to be the crowning glory of creation, holy (i.e. different, separate), blameless, pleasing to God, fulfilling his will and purposes. This is what God intended in the beginning. And it all began so well!

Each part of creation came into existence at God's command; God spoke, and it happened. And stage by stage, God created the world and the universe, and at each point he declared it to be "good!".

The writer of the book of Genesis tells us that *God saw all that he had made and it was very good.*

But you don't need a degree in theology to realise something has gone wrong. It all had such a promising start, but what would God say today? Would he look at everything now and say it is "*very good*"? Violence, hunger, murder, wars, pollution, attacks on young and old, disregard for the sanctity of life, greed, self-centredness, hatred, prejudice, and worst of all, a total disregard for

God and his claim on our lives.

We could go on, listing the ills and evils of our 21st century world, describing human corruption and failure, self-destruction, injustice and suffering. It's all very depressing when we think how it could have been, how it *should* have been, how it was *meant* to be.

But I don't think you've come here this evening to be reminded of all this. You could have stayed at home and read the Sunday papers, or watched the news on the television! I imagine you want to hear *good* news. Paul tells us that the good news is this... *God's purpose has not changed!* God's purpose in creating us in the first place has not changed. It may have been frustrated; we may have hindered God in achieving his aims. But *God's purpose has not changed!*

v 9 **God has made known to us the mystery of his will according to his good pleasure which he purposed in Christ - to be put into effect when the times will have reached their fulfilment - to bring all things in heaven and on earth together under one head, even Christ**

The Living Bible is perhaps easier to follow - **This was God's purpose - that when the time is ripe he will gather us all together from wherever we are - in heaven or on earth - to be with him in Christ for ever.** This is God's intention, and he has not yet changed his mind, and he never will!

And Paul describes here God's great work of restoration and renewal. And in the heart of what is admittedly a difficult passage of scripture, in verse 7 we see the first step. We see God's strategy, his plan. We see the grace of God at work, bringing forgiveness, breaking the chains of the past, and giving us a brand-new start. *In him (Jesus Christ) we have redemption through his blood, the forgiveness of sins, in accordance with the riches of God's grace.*

In Christ we have *redemption* and *forgiveness* – two great Bible words.

Redemption - the main idea behind this word is release, deliverance, freedom, but *at a price,* a price we ourselves could never afford. William Temple writes: *The only thing I contribute of my own is the sin from which I need to be redeemed!*

We are slaves - slaves to sin. We are held captive by the powers of evil which rule in our hearts. And if this sounds a bit over-dramatic, then remember this - evil does not always manifest itself in obvious ways with the grotesque monsters and demons of horror movies. The Devil is far more subtle in his approach and attack.

Just think of the way temptation overwhelms us sometimes. It can be a subtle process. Just think about Adam and Eve and the planting of a thought, an idea which eats away at us until we feel almost compelled to do something we know is wrong. Just think of the way we deceive selves.

We are slaves held captive by the powers of evil and by the desire to please selves. And we are powerless to break free in our own strength. We are prisoners on death row, needing to be set free. And by the *grace of God* it's possible! By the *grace of God* we can walk out of the condemned cell, out into the fresh air and sunshine, free and forgiven!

In him we have <u>redemption</u> through his blood - the <u>forgiveness</u> of sins

The second great Bible word here is *forgiveness.*

We can say a number of things about *forgiveness.* First of all, *forgiveness* is not about us changing our minds about God. It is about God changing his mind about us.

Let me give an example. Suppose a son has insulted his father. They have had a blazing row, and the son has hurled a string of verbal abuse at him, then turned his back and gone his own way. To make matters worse the son has stolen from his father, and has slandered his name in the wider community. He has generally proved himself unworthy to be called that man's son.

Suppose this son then realises he has done wrong, and is filled with genuine remorse, shame, regret. Suppose this son does all he can, all within his power to put things right. His whole attitude towards his father changes, his behaviour towards his father is transformed beyond recognition.

This isn't forgiveness, is it? It is one-sided. The effort is all on the son's part. The father may take note of this change in his son's attitude, yet still remain bitter and unrelenting, and unforgiving.

It is one thing to have a change of heart accompanied by the determination to change our ways – that is repentance. But it needs more than this. The father has to want to forgive the son.

Forgiveness is not about a change in our attitude towards God, but a change in his attitude towards us, and this is completely out of our hands.

Forgiveness is not the same thing as peace of mind, an easy conscience. The conscience is a precious gift from God, but it is only a *guide* concerning right and wrong. The conscience is now part of our fallen nature, so it is no longer reliable. It can be very flexible, and can easily be modified, fine-tuned, by the attitudes and morality of the age we live in. There are people who are hardly troubled by conscience, but who ought to be! *Forgiveness* is not about having an easy conscience.

Forgiveness does not mean we can escape the consequences of our sins and mistakes.

We may be forgiven. Our eternal destiny may be safe and secure, through Christ. We may take real comfort and encouragement in Paul's words:

There is now no condemnation for those who are in Christ Jesus. We may take real comfort and encouragement in these words, and rightly so. But nevertheless, the laws of nature and the laws of society still operate.

A drug user may bear scars long after conversion in terms of addiction and related disease. A drunken driver may still have to live with the fact that his or her foolishness has killed a child. A murderer may receive new life in Christ but is powerless to bring the victim back to life, and powerless to take away the grief, sorrow, and bitterness and hatred of the victim's relatives.

And what is true of so-called "greater" sins is true also of what we see as "lesser" sins. Lives can be damaged by our selfishness and unkindness, and, try as we may, we are not always able to repair the damage. Gossip spreads lies and half-truths and innuendo that can't be retrieved. People will go on believing there is no smoke without fire long after God has forgiven our wagging tongues.

Sins have consequences which don't necessarily evaporate with repentance and forgiveness.

What else can we say about forgiveness?

Forgiveness doesn't trivialise sin. It does not suggest that sin doesn't matter.

When *we* forgive people, we often use these very words: "It's OK, don't worry - it doesn't matter!" We may have been deeply hurt or offended, but if the person apologises, we tend to dismiss it as of no importance.

Not so with sin! After all, what is sin? It is an offence against God. Sometimes sin is an act of rebellion against God, or opposition to God. Even if the sin is committed against a fellow human, it is still an offence against God.

Look at Psalm 51, written by David, after his adultery with Bathsheba, which resulted in effect in the murder of her husband Uriah. There were at least two sins committed there – sins against people. But what does David say in Psalm 51?

Have mercy on me, O God,
according to your unfailing love;
according to your great compassion
blot out my transgressions.
Wash away all my iniquity
and cleanse me from my sin.
For I know my transgressions,
and my sin is always before me.
<u>Against you, you only,</u> have I sinned
and done what is evil in your sight,

Sins are committed against people, but they also involve breaking God's laws or commands, and offending God is never trivial and of no importance.

Sin hinders God's purposes, *and anything that*

hinders God's intention for us or for others can never be dismissed lightly.

We are talking here about the King of kings and Lord of lords, and he is not to be trifled with. This is the God and Father of our Lord Jesus Christ, the Sovereign Lord, the Creator of the universe, and when we open our eyes and recognise just who it is that we've offended, surely we will never again see wrongdoing as being trivial. God's forgiveness does not trivialise sin.

What then have we said so far?

1. *forgiveness* is not about change in our attitude towards God, but a change in his attitude towards us.

2. *forgiveness* is not the same as an easy conscience.

3. *forgiveness* does not mean we don't have to face consequences.

4. *forgiveness* does not trivialise sin.

And now fifthly, and most important perhaps...

Forgiveness is not cheap.

verse 7 - *In him we have redemption **through his blood**, the forgiveness of sins.*

God's forgiveness costs us nothing, *but it cost Jesus his life!*

The Bible does not dwell on the horror of crucifixion, and neither should we, but if we ever think forgiveness is cheap, then we should then stop and think about the cost. Humiliation. Excruciating pain. Intense thirst. Crushing pressure on the chest and lungs. And all this was suffered by Christ, God incarnate, God himself, dying the death we deserve in order that we may be forgiven.

Just one more thing we can say about *forgiveness*. There is a <u>purpose</u> in God's forgiveness.

Imagine you are in a crowded street and a stranger steps on your toe and says "Sorry", you forgive them and that's the end of it. Or perhaps you are entering a shop and the person in front lets the door go, not realising you're there. The person apologises. So you make no fuss, accept the apology and the whole thing is forgotten. The stranger is forgiven and goes on his or her way. And the chances are you will never meet again. You forgive them, *but you remain strangers.*

God's purpose is that we should not remain strangers. He does not forgive us and then send us on our way. God's forgiveness has an aim.

Forgiveness arises out of the grace of God, the loving heart of the Father. It is for the express purpose of restoring our relationship, making the way clear for us to become sons and daughters of the living God, removing all the barriers in the way.

When the Queen (or nowadays the King) grants a Royal Pardon, the prisoner does not move into Buckingham Palace. He or she does not become a member of the royal family. He does not have a place set at the royal dining table, not even once. There isn't even likely to be an invitation to a Garden Party in the palace grounds.

But when God forgives, it's so that his love can flow into our lives. It's so that we can be adopted into his family, so that he can share our daily lives.

Look again at what Paul says: *In him (Jesus Christ) we have redemption through his blood, the forgiveness of sins, in accordance with the riches of God's grace that he lavished upon us.*

So, we see those two important and significant words in this verse – *redemption* and *forgiveness*.

There are two more very important words that we need to notice. We find them at the beginning of v 7 *"in him"*.

We find a similar construction over and over again in the passage...

v 3 *"in Christ"*
v 4 "*in him*"
v 6 *"in the one he loves"*
v 9 *"in Christ"*

It means "in a real, living union with Christ". Redemption and forgiveness are rooted first of all in a relationship with Jesus Christ. To say **we have redemption through the blood of Christ** is not the whole gospel message.

<u>IN HIM</u> **we have redemption through his blood.** When our heart, mind, will, and spirit are united with Christ and when our whole life is in harmony with Christ, then we are back on course, back where we belong.

This is God's real aim. This is God's purpose.

What is the meaning of life?
What's it all about?
What are we here for?
What's the purpose behind it all?

Here's Paul's answer - our purpose is *to be adopted as his children, God's heirs, through Jesus Christ, in accordance with his pleasure and will.*

And this is only made possible through the salvation and forgiveness that are ours because of Christ's death on the cross.

EPHESIANS 1:15FF

Two brothers lived in a particular town where they were involved in corruption, deceit and every manner of vice. In fact, rumour had it that they were connected in some way with some very famous organised crime families as well.

In the course of their criminal activities, both brothers accumulated a considerable amount of wealth.

When the older brother died, the townspeople were not exactly grief-stricken, but his brother wanted to honour his older brother and partner in crime, so he planned an elaborate funeral. The problem was finding a minister who was willing to conduct the service. After all, neither of them had ever attended a church service.

Knowing that one of the local churches was in the midst of a fundraising campaign for some much-needed repairs, the younger brother called upon the minister.

"Reverend," he said, "I know my brother and I never attended your church, or any church for that matter. I also know that you've probably heard a lot of things about my brother and me, but I'd like you to conduct his funeral. And if you'll say he was a saint, I'll write you a cheque for £50,000. That'll go a long way to repairing the church roof."

After some thought, the minister agreed to conduct the service, but he had one condition. The £50,000 had to be paid in advance. And so it was.

On the day of the funeral, the church was packed. Curiosity brought dozens of people in, who were certainly not there to honour the rich man, but who wanted to hear what the minister would actually say. The rest of the crowd was made up of the gangsters and criminals the brothers had associated with.

The service began with the usual readings, hymns and prayers. And then it was time for the address.

The minister began slowly, but then step by step launched into a catalogue of the terrible things the elder brother had done, how he had been selfish, greedy, corrupt, caring about no one but himself, womanising, drinking excessively, and on and on.

The younger brother, sitting there in the front pew was getting angrier and angrier that the minister wasn't fulfilling his promise, but during the service there wasn't much he could do about it.

Finally, after about ten minutes the minister concluded his sermon by saying: "Yes my friends, this man was a no-good, dirty, rotten scoundrel! But, compared to his brother, he was a saint!"

The minister was, of course, using the word "saint" in the way many people think about saints.

When we hear the word "saint" we usually think of people like St. Francis, St. Teresa, St. Catherine, St. Bernadette, or St. Ignatius of Loyola, or at the very least, St Matthew, St Mark, St Luke, St John, St Paul and so on. We usually tend to think of a saint as someone whose life and faith has been tested according to specific standards and criteria, and who has been found to be just short of perfect, flawless.

Certainly to become a saint in the Roman Catholic tradition, one has to follow a set procedure and tick all the boxes on the checklist.

But this is not what Paul has in mind when he addresses this letter to *the saints that are in Ephesus*, (although the latest edition of the NIV renders the word "hagios" as "God's holy people") and when here in v 15 he refers to their love for all the saints (NIV – God's people").

This usage of the word is not so much about people whose lives and faith *have been* tested; but is more about people whose lives *were being* tested at that time. And these people were not called saints according to some set procedure as such, but tested against the standards of the gospel and the word of God.

In the New Testament, saints are people who are an example to others of devotion to Christ; people who, because of their faith in Christ show something of the light of Christ in their lives.

I am reminded of the story of the little girl who was fascinated by the stained-glass windows in her church, depicting various traditional saints. She was asked if she knew what a saint was, and her reply was "Saints are people who the light shines through."

I think she was right there – people through whom the light of Christ shines. It may be their humility showing Christ's humility. It may be their attitude when troubles and difficulties or suffering come along, and the way such circumstances drive them closer to God. It may be that other aspects of their life and faith show something of Christ and his influence upon them, and his power within them. It may be their care for other people, their love, their compassion.

Saints are people who, because of their faith in Christ, show something of the light of Christ in their lives, and this makes them different. This is, in fact, what saints are – people whom God has made holy, different, separated from unbelievers.

And Paul here gives thanks for such people, and he prays for them. What does he pray?

I think Paul was aware of a common danger for believers and his prayer takes account of this. What is the danger? The danger is that we come to faith in Christ, we accept Jesus Christ as our Lord and Saviour, and, whilst we may serve him and the church in practical ways, and, whilst we may be unwavering in our faith, and we may even bring others to faith by our witness - whilst we can say all this, there's a sense in which we stand still at the point where it matters most.

Let's see what Paul prays for and perhaps we'll begin to understand what I mean.

In the preceding verses Paul writes of the riches of the grace of God in Christ. And in the previous chapter of this book, we focussed on two words in particular - redemption and forgiveness.

We didn't really touch on it, but Paul was getting carried away with the whole idea of being chosen by God, called by God, predestined. And he was so excited, so caught up in the wonder of it all, that he couldn't stop piling word upon word, thought upon thought as he tried his very best to do justice to the riches of God's grace in Christ. In the Greek Paul writes a sentence with more than 200 words in it, and he was struggling to put an end to the sentence.

Why? Because, for all the words, Paul knew that he was trying to put into words something that simply can't be put into words, something that transcends human language. This might, in fact, explain why we often find Paul's writings so difficult!

And now we find him praying a prayer that the believers in Ephesus (and us) would understand all that he's been trying to describe.

Human language can never describe adequately the glory of Christ. At best, it's all just words. At worst, Paul leaves us frowning as we're left trying to understand what he is actually saying!

Perhaps Paul realises this. And he longs for us somehow to grasp, to see, to find what Paul himself has found in Christ Jesus. So he prays that the God of our Lord Jesus Christ - the glorious Father - would give the saints in Ephesus *the Spirit of wisdom and revelation.*

Why? - *so that they may know God better.*

Paul then goes on to add some detail as to what he means, and he speaks of **hope** and a glorious **inheritance,** and God's incomparably great **power.**

I don't pretend to understand all that he says here but at the very least I can see this - that none of us will really get to know God better without God's help. We need the *Spirit of wisdom and revelation -*

"revelation" being the unveiling of things we could never discover by ourselves.

What Paul most desires is that all believers would experience in their hearts and lives the wonder and thrill of knowing God better. This isn't achieved just by applying the intellect. Despite what people say, it *is* about feelings! It's about knowing God, not simply knowing about God. It's about a relationship, not simply building up an encyclopaedic knowledge about God. It's about experiencing Jesus - the joy and peace and grace and love and mercy found in him.

I am sure Paul's prayer first and foremost is that all believers will feel this. That they will experience this (what we might almost call the "Wow Factor"), even if we can't understand it or explain it or describe it.

After all - head knowledge can be argued out of us by so-called human logic and reason. Experience and a relationship can't be taken away quite so easily.

I recall when I was at college, where I found the second year of study the toughest. It wasn't so much that I struggled with the academic work. It was the challenge of the atheist philosophies we were having to engage with in Christian apologetics.

Some atheist arguments are quite compelling and

could have rocked my faith, as they did, in fact, with some other students, were it not for the fact that deep within I had an experience and a relationship that defied all their arguments.

It's like music, sunsets, delicious food. We could, if we wished. describe these logically, intellectually, but if we did, we would have missed the point. To describe a fine wine in terms of aldehydes, ketones, esters, acid content, tannin and so on is to miss the point.

A musical score could be described as a mathematical representation of music, or the music could be represented on an oscilloscope or using other scientific equipment. But you can't beat being surrounded by the sound of a full orchestra in full flow.

We can describe the chemical reaction that takes place when we bite into a lemon and the acid interacts with the taste buds, but we have to experience it to really know how that feels.

And we can describe God theologically, listing his attributes, his creative and redemptive work. We can speak of God's grace, his love, his mercy, his power, his holiness and so on, but unless we experience God for ourselves, we won't really know him.

Paul prays that the saints at Ephesus and all believers may know God better by experiencing

God in the context of a living relationship.

He then prays that knowing God better will include three things that are the result of, as Paul puts it - *the eyes of your heart being enlightened* - which I take to mean the control centre, the heart and mind, being informed by these three things.

First - v 18 *the hope to which God has called you.*

Hope is not just about the future. It's about *having* a future, and for believers the future stretches from here to eternity!

Some people seem to have no present worth speaking of and definitely no hope for the future. They seem to be trapped in circumstances or in a lifestyle, and can see no way out, no escape.

People are trapped in modern forms of slavery today, and in seemingly hopeless situations, including people who are in bondage to addictions, or life on the margins of society.

Paul prays that as believers we will know, feel, sense, experience the joy and the thrill of the hope to which God has called us.

In 1 Thess 5:23 – Paul writes: *May God himself, the God of peace, sanctify you through and through. May your whole spirit, soul and body be kept blameless at the coming of our Lord Jesus Christ. The one who calls you is faithful and he will do it.*

And in Philippians 1:6 - he writes... *being confident of this, that he who began a good work in you will carry it on to completion until the day of Christ Jesus.*

This is the hope to which God has called us.

And then Paul prays that they would also know the *riches of God's glorious inheritance in the saints.*

What do you think of when you think of an inheritance? Some rich uncle or aunt leaving you a fortune? Not all inheritances work out that way. For example, a Philadelphia woman apparently left her divorced husband $1 to buy a rope to hang himself!

To some extent, inheritances reflect what the benefactor thinks of the beneficiary. and with God it is no different.

The language used suggests God thinks a lot of us - *the riches of God's glorious inheritance in the saints*

For some people, riches simply mean material possessions, and they can't see beyond what they can touch and feel and possess in some way or other.

Money and wealth and material possession can easily have a powerful influence and hold on our lives, the reason being that they give us an illusion of security. It is so much easier to trust in what we can see and touch and feel than to trust in some intangible idea or promise.

Paul prays that we will be able to know, to trust, in these intangible but no less real riches, to experience them , to be assured of them.

We can't see and touch and feel them in a sensory way, but they are ours nonetheless.

The fullness of these riches may again transcend human language, but we can at least say this. If these riches come from the creator of heaven and earth, we can be sure of this. They are worth more than the sum total of all the material wealth in the universe.

the riches of God's glorious inheritance in the saints

Paul also prays that they may know, experience God's *incomparably great power.*

To live our lives as God intends, we need a power beyond our own power. Human nature, human weakness is such that we struggle and fail no matter how hard we try, but Paul says God's power is available for us.

Dynamite and even nuclear energy harnessed in atomic bombs is nothing compared with the real power behind this universe! We can't really begin to imagine, let alone describe the limitless power of God.

Paul says this power is available to us. I can barely grasp what that means, so Paul says, if we really want to know what it's like, it's like the power that raised Jesus from the dead! Such power is simply beyond human comprehension.

God's power is creative power. It is not the destructive power of earthquakes and volcanoes but creative power - God's *incomparably great power.*

It is the power behind the incarnation, behind the healing sick people, the opening of the eyes of the blind, the cleansing of lepers, the casting out of demons, raising the dead, and defeating death. And Paul says this power is available to us, limited only by the paucity of our faith!

God's Word through Paul declares that, with God's *incomparably great* power, we have the strength to live in God's way. I think I can at least grasp that and what it means!

It means that "we're only human" is no longer a valid excuse, since in Christ, who was and is fully human as well as fully God, we see the potential, the true heights human flesh can reach, and Paul prays that we will come to realise this; that we will experience for ourselves God's *incomparably great power* as he himself had done, most notably on the Road to Damascus, but I imagine Paul would say he experienced this on a daily basis, and we can too.

Our house, just like your house, is wired for electricity, electrical power. How do I know? Because when I flick a switch, the light comes on. When I plug the washing machine in, or the computer, or the vacuum cleaner or the Black and Decker drill, or the TV or radio, power is available.

The thing is that the power is available all the time, but I need to plug in and switch on.

Faith is the switch. Only as we begin to see by faith who we are in Christ, and who**se** we are in Christ, and what we have in Christ, can we begin to live in God's power and strength and not our own.

In Philippians 3:10 Paul says: *I want to know Christ and the power of his resurrection.*

And Paul wants us to know God's *incomparably great power* too.

So there we have it - Paul's prayer for the saints in Ephesus, and for all believers, including us.

We live in a world that likes to see results. With all this going for us, perhaps the world is entitled to see some results in us and all believers, results in the form of a greater impact that comes from knowing God better, and growing in our *knowledge and experience of Christ* [1]

---

[1] This phrase was part of the Vision Statement of the church I served in prior to retirement. *We are*

here to honour the Lord Jesus Christ, to grow in our knowledge and love of him, and to share his love in our town, nation and world.

EPHESIANS 2:1-10

Some time ago, an American newspaper surveyed personnel directors of the nation's largest companies for their most unusual experiences when they were interviewing people for jobs. You'll be amazed at some of the things that actually happened during those job interviews.

For some strange reason one job applicant challenged the interviewer to arm wrestle!

A balding candidate excused himself during the interview and then returned wearing a full hairpiece.

One candidate wore earphones to the interview and, when asked to remove them, explained that it was OK. She could listen to the interviewer and the music at the same time.

Another said she hadn't had time for lunch, so started to eat a hamburger and fries in the interviewer's office.

One applicant interrupted the questioning to phone her therapist for advice.

And another dozed off during the interview.

I don't expect any of these people were successful in being offered employment! They wouldn't stand a chance, I am sure. Their behaviour was discourteous, insensitive, hopeless, clueless. None of us would act like that, would we?

But just a minute! That is what Paul says we were like, not in terms of trying to get work but in terms of our relationship with God!

We were hopeless, clueless, maybe even disrespectful, and as he puts it, *lifeless! Dead!* And the problem with being dead is that there is nothing you can do about it. You are powerless!

As for you, you were dead... he says here in Ephesians 2:1

Paul is addressing these words to Gentiles but goes on to include himself and his fellow Jews in v 3 as he describes what we might call the human problem.

Nostalgia is a condition that affects a certain age group and is, I suspect, on the increase as we baby boomers pass through the system. Just think about the number of books published about the good old days. Or CDs (OK – so we've moved on now with MP3s and streaming music on the internet!). Among our CDs is one of "Housewives' Favourites" from the 50s! And another - Mairzy Doats and other great comic songs from the 30's and 40's! I wasn't even born until the late 40s!

What on earth am I doing with such CDs? Nostalgia. That's what it is, even though I have to say I didn't actually buy those CDs – it was more to do with having a wife who worked in a museum with a shop.

We also have books at home covering every decade since I don't know when. And the internet has a limitless supply of resources from the past.

But here Paul brings us face to face with the reality of one aspect of our past, and it doesn't fill us with nostalgia. He gives a brutally honest description of what we were before we accepted Christ as Lord and Saviour.

As for you, you were <u>dead</u> in your transgressions and sins,

transgressions – the Greek word means to stumble, slip, fall and obviously refers to a moral fall.

sins here translates a Greek word that means to miss the mark, to fall short of the target, to fail to make the grade.

At the end of v 2 Paul uses a word that sums up the main problem – *disobedience* - and, he says, it's all to do with *satisfying the cravings of our sinful nature.* It's about a life centred on the priorities of the world, and driven by an appetite for pleasure in all its forms. "Self-indulgence" sums it up – we tend to be driven by self-indulgence.

But, we may say, *I'm not all that bad and I never was as bad as the picture Paul paints. Some people have done much worse things than I've ever done!*

Or I look at my neighbours. They don't seem like wicked, evil people but ordinary, decent folk.

What are we saying then? That Christ didn't need to die on the cross as far as we or they are concerned? That Jesus didn't need to go to all that trouble for our sakes?

The Bible says that it isn't about comparing ourselves with other people; it's about comparing ourselves with God who is pure and holy, righteous, perfect.

It doesn't matter how moral and upright we may have been, before we accepted Christ, we were trapped on death row, separated from God, and unresponsive to the breadth and depth of his love.

As far as God is concerned, our petty sins, and the sins of the most evil, depraved person who's ever lived, were equally enough to require the death of Christ on the cross.

And I am afraid the result is doom and gloom!

It has to be if we are (or were) "*objects of wrath*" which means under God's righteous anger, God's judgement, God's condemnation, anger, judgement, condemnation rooted firmly in God's holiness, righteousness and justice.

Understand this though. It isn't God's will that any should perish. Let me remind you not only of John 3:16 but the verses that follow... *God so loved the world that he gave his one and only Son, that whoever believes in him shall not perish but have eternal life.* We all are quite familiar with this verse, but don't hear very often what follows. *For God did not send his Son into the world to condemn the world, but to save the world through him. Whoever believes in him is not condemned, but whoever does not believe stands condemned already because he has not believed in the name of God's one and only Son.*

By their disobedience and rejection of Christ, people condemn themselves. We are condemned by our own actions, our own unbelief.

What a depressing picture of the human condition! What a gloomy depressing picture... until you read on. Verse 4 and the verses that follow have- been described as a *beacon of light and hope in a sea of despair.* The reason is found in the first two words of v 4 which in the original Greek read "*But God*".

That short word. "but" is almost always a

significant and important word in scripture because it indicates a contrast. Add another short word - "*God*" – and together the short phrase becomes even more significant. It reminds us that God has intervened and done what we are powerless to do.

We *were* dead. Lifeless, and therefore helpless, powerless and hopeless. We couldn't even appeal against the sentence; we couldn't claim we are innocent of the charges against us. Death doesn't allow for any appeal! We were helpless, powerless and hopeless.

"***But God...*** " or as the NIV puts it: ___But___ *because of his great love for us,* ___God___*, who is rich in mercy, made us alive with Christ even when we were dead in transgressions--it is by grace you have been saved.*

Love is the reason why God is merciful and gracious and made us alive - *because of his great love for us.* God is love - it's his nature and so he can't help being compassionate and merciful towards us.

God loves us. He hates the sin, detests it, but this does not mean he hates us. Because of his great love, God is always seeking out the very best for us. And he loves us here and now - just as we are - but he loves us so much that he does not want to leave us just as we are.

Paul says God is also *"rich in mercy"* - the word

translated here as "rich" also means "abundant, opulent, extravagant". *"God who is **extravagant** in mercy"*.

"Mercy" is a negative version of "grace" - if *grace* means treating us as we **don't** deserve to be treated, *mercy* means *not* treating us as we deserve to be treated.

It is by grace you have been saved – i.e. not because we have done anything to deserve it. What we do deserve is eternal punishment, eternal separation from God, and from the reach of his loving kindness, but God, in his mercy, hasn't given us what we deserve. He's given us what we don't deserve - salvation, new life in Christ.

*...**because of his great love for us, God, who is rich in mercy, made us <u>alive</u> with Christ.***

It's summed up neatly in v 8 - ***For it is by grace you have been saved, through faith--and this not from yourselves, it is the gift of God-- not by works, so that no one can boast.***

There are two ways by which people can attempt to be saved - on God's terms or our own. Our own plan of salvation is based on works of some kind or other, and some make valiant attempts at earning salvation. I would even go so far as to say that the world is in some ways a better place because of their endeavours.

So some try the path of good works, trying to do

enough to balance the scales by endeavouring to make sure their good works outweigh their sins.

Others are more inward looking and try to earn salvation by some form of self-discipline or by punishing themselves in some way.

Some time ago I was looking round the cathedral at Amiens in Northern France, and I saw there, set in the tiles on the floor in the centre of the nave a labyrinth marked out.

You don't have to go as far as France. There is one not too far away out in the open in the village of Wing near Rutland Water. (*I was preaching in my last church in Kettering*).

Labyrinths are usually medieval, providing a form of pilgrimage for those who could not afford a long journey, or who were too old or infirm to make such a journey.

This much shorter journey was usually made on their knees as they moved along the markings of the labyrinth, crawling round and stopping now and then for prayer and meditation at set points.

For some this would be a sincere spiritual exercise, but for others it would be an attempt at earning favour with God.

Other people may look to other forms of religious ritual. Baptism for example, or confirmation, or taking communion regularly, or joining a church, regular attendance at services.

None of these is wrong. That's why they're called <u>good</u> works. But they can be no more than attempts at earning favour with God.

The main problem with trying to earn salvation by good works is that we can never do enough to make ourselves acceptable to God, especially since the core of the problem is a sinful nature which we are powerless to change.

The other way is, of course, *God's* way - *by grace through faith.*

There is a sense it's still by works, but not ours! We are saved by *Christ's* work on the cross on that first Good Friday as he bore the penalty, the punishment for our sins so that justice could be done.

1 Peter 2:24 - *He himself bore our sins in his body on the tree, so that we might die to sins and live for righteousness; by his wounds you have been healed.*

It is by grace you have been saved, through faith -

Faith isn't about intellectual knowledge. I would even venture to suggest that faith is not just about belief. Faith is about believing in something or someone enough for it to make a difference in our lives. And Paul says that such faith is even God's gift for us.

The question is: *why does God go to all this trouble?* And I think that the usual evangelical answer with its emphasis on the individual can mislead us here.

God doesn't go to all this trouble just to make it possible for us to be forgiven, saved, have peace with God. So what is the purpose of the gospel?

Let me offer two reasons why God goes to all this trouble.

The first reason is found in vv 6,7 ***God raised us up with Christ and seated us with him in the heavenly realms in Christ Jesus, <u>in order that in the coming ages he might show the incomparable riches of his grace, expressed in his kindness to us in Christ Jesus.</u>***

Traditionally the word "*trophy*" has been used but this may offer a wrong image - the head of a stag mounted on the wall of a stately home, or some other big game trophy. The image of the head of a dead animal may come to mind with the word "trophy", so it is not a very helpful image anymore than a silver trophy or cup would be.

The idea here is of us - *saved by grace through faith* - being evidence for all to see - evidence of the power of God's grace, mercy and love. We can be the means by which God reveals something of his nature and power.

We can tend to underestimate such power.

When Spurgeon was preaching on the power of God needed to convert a soul, he said this...

"If Niagara could suddenly be made to leap upward instead of forever dashing downward from it's rocky height, it were not such a miracle as to change the perverse will and raging passions of men...

Conversion is a work comparable to the making of a world. He only who fashioned the heavens and the earth could create a new nature. It is a work that is not to be paralleled, it is unique and unrivalled, seeing that Father, Son, and Spirit must all cooperate in it; for to implant the new nature in the Christian, there must be the decree of the eternal Father, the death of the ever-blessed Son, and the fullness of the operation of the adorable Spirit.

It is a mighty deed. The labours of Hercules were but trifles compared to this... child's play compared with renewing a right spirit in the fallen nature of man."

And we provide the living evidence for all to see. We are not dead, lifeless trophies but living proof that God's grace, mercy and love are incredibly powerful.

Another writer puts it like this - *In bringing us from a position of death and depravity to one of deliverance, God has performed a miracle of the magnitude of the creating of a world. He has totally transformed us at the core of our being by giving us a new nature.*

Imagine you were called by one of those beauty

businesses which specialises in "make-overs." Imagine if they offered you a free "make-over". How would you feel? Would you be flattered? Or perhaps even insulted!

Well, let me say this. No beauty business is going to advertise its work by selecting a beautiful woman and then making only slight improvements on her beauty. They are going to take the most hopeless case they can find, and then take the credit for the transformation.

Or if a plastic surgeon called you, offering you free cosmetic surgery, so that he could use you for advertising, you may feel grateful, but not proud. He wouldn't be choosing people for their good looks, but so that he could demonstrate his skills as a plastic surgeon!

So it is with God's grace. God sent Jesus Christ to the world, to suffer and to die in our place. He did this because we were in such a hopeless situation. He did it so that he could demonstrate his grace, and his power in transforming a "dead" man or woman into a living testimony of his grace and power.

God's motivation in saving us doesn't exactly flatter us, but it does glorify Him. That's one reason why God goes to all this trouble – to demonstrate the power of his love, grace and mercy.

We find the second reason there in v 10 - *we are God's workmanship*. The Greek word there is *poema* which means a work of art, a masterpiece.

Creation itself is a work of art. Such a great work of art that even when it is a fallen, broken creation, through Adam's sin, it is still wonderful and beautiful. I don't know about you but I'm always amazed at the intricate and detailed design of just about everything - stars, mountains, lakes, butterflies, flowers. These are all the results of God's creative genius and power. From a grain of sand or a snowflake to the Swiss Alps or Niagara Falls, we just have to marvel at the mind that could conceive these things, and the kind of power that could create them.

But out of the whole of creation, what is God's masterpiece? Well, if you want to see something really special, take a look at a newborn baby. The design of the human body is incredible. But human beings aren't God's masterpiece, not according to what Paul says here.

God's masterpiece, work of art, is not just a human being but a human being who has been *made alive in Christ*.

The pinnacle of creation isn't the human race as such - *we are God's workmanship, created in Christ Jesus*

Those of us who are **created in Christ Jesus** are

God's masterpiece. And the reason why God has gone to all this trouble is so that we can be his masterpiece, *created in Christ Jesus to do good works, which God prepared in advance for us to do.*

You see, there **is** a place for good works after all! Someone once said: *"true Christianity is a faith filled with good works"* but not good works as a <u>means</u> of earning salvation, but rather good works that <u>accompany</u> salvation, good works which God himself has prepared for us to do.

A minister was walking past an old Victorian house one day when he noticed a small boy trying to ring the doorbell but the boy was too short - the doorbell was high up. The boy kept jumping as high as he could but he couldn't reach the button.

The minister saw here an opportunity to do a good work and he stepped up and rang the doorbell several times. "And now what young man?" he said to the young boy.

"Now," said the boy, "we run as fast as we can!"

God certainly hadn't prepared that good work!

When **we** decide to do good works, we can sometimes get it wrong. But God already has areas of service in mind for us, and our task is to discover the areas of service he has prepared.

It may be a matter of trial and error, but one thing certain, if we don't try, we won't discover what

God has in mind for us to do.

It means we need to be open and actively seeking guidance in terms of the general area of service, and what this means in practice on a daily basis, is not so much asking the usual question - *what would Jesus do?* The problem with WWJD? is that it suggests Jesus is absent from our daily life.

We should be asking *what does Jesus want to do through me?*

We are God's workmanship, created in Christ Jesus to do good works, which God prepared in advance for us to do.

Well, we've come a long way! We started out on death row and have ended up in an art gallery as God's works of art, God's masterpiece.

The irony is that when we are on death row, we don't realise it till we are saved! And that's how it is for many people today - people who sometimes tell us we should "get a life!", people who believe they are the ones who are living life to the full.

Paul's word for them is that they are **dead** - lifeless and therefore humanly speaking helpless, powerless, hopeless.

The good news that we have somehow to find ways of sharing is this. No one is helpless and powerless and hopeless; it's just that they need help and power and a hope that lies outside of themselves and their own efforts, and that the grace, mercy and love we have experienced is theirs too if they'll only ask God for the gift of faith to enable them to reach out and receive all God wants to give them.

And if they won't pray, then it is up to us to do their praying for them, so that they too can become God's works of art.

EPHESIANS 2:11-22

Sometimes, when we are on holiday and the rain is beating down on the caravan roof, and streaming down the windows, we have found ourselves watching daytime TV, watching one of those house buying programmes such as "Homes Under the Hammer". I wouldn't normally go out of my way to watch such programmes, or daytime TV of any kind, but it is a different matter when you are cooped up in a caravan on a wet day.

This kind of programme is not really my cup of tea, but nevertheless I am fascinated by the way they have a tendency to draw you in once you start to watch.

One thing I have noticed is this. People seem to be more interested in knocking walls down in their houses than they are in building walls. And yet, in the rest of life the opposite is often true. People, perhaps without even realising it, tend to build walls or fences rather than demolish them. There are walls of division everywhere we look.

Think of all the conflict in the world, currently (2024) with Israel and the Hamas terrorists in Gaza, reflecting barriers between Israelis and Palestinians. In 2002, Israel started constructing a wall, slicing through Palestinian communities, agricultural fields, and farmland, such that Bethlehem is a divided city, as is Jerusalem.

The Israel West Bank barrier is a wall built by the State of Israel to separate Palestinian territories from Israel. It is built mostly of fences and in some places, it is built of high concrete walls. There is even a wall along the middle of a highway, separating Palestinian traffic from Israeli traffic – dubbed the "apartheid road".

Then there is the continuing conflict between Russia and Ukraine, in fact, Russia and the Western nations.

When he was President, Donald Trump wanted to build a wall on the Mexican border to keep Mexicans out of the United States.

And, of course, there is the UK's withdrawal from the European Union, creating trade, social and cultural barriers.

Walls of division are to be found in every part of the world, and in many different areas of society. And we ourselves are not immune. Wherever there's an "us and them" situation, whether intentional or not, then we have a wall of division, albeit invisible. It may be about politics, religion, social class, culture, appearances, skin colour, values, concerns, tastes, age and so on. There are many walls that divide us, that separate us from "them", whoever "they" may be.

These walls may be built by **pride,** believing we are better than others. While few would say such a thing in so many words, we may imply it in our words and attitudes. Pride (and its close partner - prejudice) builds walls. **Superiority** builds walls, as also does a feeling of **inferiority.**

Do you recall that occasion when Jesus met a Samaritan woman at a well ? She had built a wall of **inferiority** between herself and Jesus, on at least two counts - she was a Samaritan and a woman. But Jesus looked over the wall and dismantled it brick by brick, contrary to the tendency of most Jews at that time to maintain the wall.

Fear and insecurity can build walls, along with many other human feelings or characteristics. Walls that divide; walls that separate **us** from **them.**

There are even hints of such walls here in this passage in Ephesians 2 - "**you**" meaning Gentiles, and "**we**" meaning Jews. But Paul only draws this distinction to make a point about such walls of division.

Now, if I was to stand here and say that I've the

solution to all this division and hostility, I suspect you might not believe me. And yet this is the essence of Paul's message to the Ephesians here in these verses.

v 14 for example... *"He himself is our peace, who has made the two one and has destroyed the barrier, the dividing wall of hostility."*

Paul was, of course, a Jew. For Jews -there were, and probably still are, only two kinds of people in the world - **us** and **them**, **Jews** and **Gentiles**, those who are described as near to God, the Jews, and those who are far away from God, the Gentiles, the rest of us.

As far as Jews were concerned, Gentiles were right at the bottom of the ladder. They believed that God created Gentiles to be fuel for the fires of Hell! They maintained a vicious hatred, a deep prejudice against all who stood outside of the Jewish nation.

But Paul's writings aren't prompted by hatred and prejudice. All he is doing is stating the sad truth, the condition of Gentiles without Christ. And what does he say?

(verse 12) *Remember that at that time you were separate from Christ, excluded from citizenship in Israel and foreigners to the covenants of the promise, without hope and without God in the world.*

-*"... you were separate from Christ..."*

What does he mean by this? "**Christ**" is, of course, not simply a name. It is a Greek word meaning *"Anointed One", "Messiah"*. And what Paul is saying here is that they - the Gentiles - had no concept of a Messiah. They had no hope of a Messiah, no expectation. For them history simply went round in circles. They had nothing to look forward to, no light at the end of the tunnel, no anticipation of a day when injustice and inequality and oppression would come to an end.

At least the Jews had a hope, a vision for the future. At least they had God's promise of an end to all that is evil, all that opposes God's purposes for the world. For them history is linear, moving towards an end.

The Jews may not have recognised the Messiah when he was standing there staring them in the face, but at least they had this hope to sustain them.

But the Gentiles lived in darkness, with no concept or hope of a Messiah. That's what *"separate from Christ"* really means.

What else does Paul say?

- *"... excluded from citizenship in Israel and foreigners to the covenants of the promise..."*

They were *outsiders.* They didn't belong. They probably didn't <u>want</u> to belong! But whether they liked it or not Gentiles were outsiders. They were not the chosen people, special to God.

Paul also says, they were **without hope,** not just without the hope of a Messiah, but without any hope at all. And they were **without God**. Actually they had many gods but were ignorant of the one true God, the Living God.

So much for the Gentiles, camped, as it were, on one hill. What about the Jews camped on the opposite hill?

It seems they had everything going for them. They possessed all that the Gentiles lacked. They looked for the coming of the Messiah. They were chosen by God so that he might reveal himself to them, and establish a special relationship with them. History as they saw it had a direction, an aim. It didn't go round in circles as far as they were concerned; it was moving towards a day of fulfilment. And they knew God, the Living God.

So, we have these two classes of people - **Jews** and **Gentiles** - with a wall of hostility and prejudice separating them. Two groups of people as different as chalk and cheese. And any reconciliation between them was out of the question. It was impossible.

There are, of course, barriers, divisions, walls that separate people today. The colour of a person's skin, cultural differences, social differences, financial differences, political differences, religious differences, or even within a religion Catholics and Protestants, Free Church or Established Church, evangelicals and liberals. And even between strict, narrow evangelicals and more open evangelicals.

And there are the very real and life-threatening divisions in many parts of the world.

What does it take to heal these divisions? It seems impossible, doesn't it? And we can't imagine the barriers, the dividing walls ever coming down. And if we are honest, we hardly dare believe anything can ever change.

Having said this - we have seen great progress in the past 30 years, with the collapse of the Soviet Union at the end of the 1980s, even though President Putin is doing his best to create division and hostility at the moment.

We had the literal dismantling of the Berlin Wall in 1989, or thereabouts. And Northern Ireland is relatively calm nowadays, even though there's always the risk of a new wall, a hard border being created. At one time it looked like there was no possible solution to the conflict there in Northern Ireland. We never dreamt we'd see Ian Paisley and Martin McGuinness sitting next to each other and sharing a joke. In fact we never imagined even seeing Ian Paisley smile!

But by and large we can't imagine all the barriers, the dividing walls ever coming down.

What does Paul say about the impossible situation between the Jews and the Gentiles? What does he say about that deep rooted hostility between the Jewish people and the rest of the world, the hostility that operates in both directions - not just from the Jews against Gentiles, but in just about every society right throughout the course of history, there has been a dislike for Jews.

Paul says - … *once you were separate from Christ, you were excluded, you had no hope and no God…*

<u>*but*</u>…

It's that significant little word '*but*', isn't it? Earlier in this chapter Paul paints a dark, gloomy picture of the human condition when he says *All of us gratified the cravings of our flesh and followed its desires and thoughts. Like the rest, we were by nature deserving of God's wrath…* and then Paul shines a beacon of light and hope into that darkness with this short word "*but*".
But because of his great love for us, God who is rich in mercy, made us alive with Christ even when we were dead in transgressions.

Sometimes it's these short words that have great significance. Watch out for them as you read your Bible because it usually means God is going to, or has, changed the situation, and he does it again here.

... you were separate from Christ, excluded from citizenship in Israel and foreigners to the covenants of the promise, without hope and without God in the world, <u>but now</u> in Christ Jesus you who once were far away have been brought near through the blood of Christ.

No longer are they separate from Christ but they are described as *in Christ Jesus.* Before they hadn't even shared the Jewish hope of a Messiah, but now they are in this personal, living relationship. They have fellowship with the Messiah, Christ Jesus.

Notice that - Christ <u>Jesus</u>. Not just "Christ". Not just the Messiah who was part of the Jewish hope, part of the expectation, part of the future, but *Christ <u>Jesus</u>.* The hope and dream of a Messiah has become embodied in the man Jesus, Christ Jesus who had come, lived and died.

And his death was not simply the meaningless end of all his fine words and good intentions. Jesus' death has meaning and purpose and has accomplished something. And they – both Jews **and** Gentiles - had entered into the benefits of his death.

Christ Jesus. Saviour - that's what "Jesus" means. The saviour of the world, both Jews and Gentiles.

Paul says, "You *have been* brought near". Again, this speaks of salvation, but it's salvation here and now as well as a hope for the future.

The prophecy of Isa 57:19 had come true – *"Peace, peace, to those far and near", says the LORD. "And I will heal them."*

It is the promise of peace - shalom - to both near and far, Jew and Gentile, fulfilled in Christ Jesus.

And in this peace and salvation Jew and Gentile become one

He himself is our peace, who has made the two one and has destroyed the barrier, the dividing wall of hostility.

Both Paul and the Ephesians had themselves experienced a transformation, a conversion. They had received the gift of peace with God, and through peace with God they had found peace with each other by the grace of God in Christ Jesus.

They themselves could give personal testimony to the power of God in Christ. They could testify that in him, the impossible had been achieved. the barrier, the dividing wall of hostility has been broken down.

In fact, two barriers had been broken down. Two significant barriers.

In the temple there was a stone wall bearing an inscription written in Greek and Latin, forbidding Gentiles from proceeding further, on pain of death. It was a physical barrier separating Jews and Gentiles. But there was another barrier in the Temple too - the curtain in front of the Holy of Holies. This was a barrier symbolising man's separation, alienation, from God.

One barrier representing the dividing wall between one group of people and another. The other representing the dividing wall between all people and God. And Christ died to destroy both.

His purpose was to create in himself one new man out of the two, thus making peace, and in this one body to reconcile both of them - Jew and Gentile - to God through the cross.

What Paul is saying is this: *the effects of the death of Christ reach far deeper and far wider than the salvation of individuals.*

You and I must, of course, come and kneel at the foot of the cross and receive forgiveness and salvation. We must, of course, repent, and believe and receive. But as we kneel at the cross and look around us, what do we find? We find others kneeling there too. We find others sharing this same need of God's mercy, and God's grace. We find others sharing this same sense of weakness and failure. We find others also seeking and receiving forgiveness.

We find that what saves us is not that we've kept all the rules and regulations, and done the right things in our lives, attending Sunday School and church since our earliest days. We find that race, sex, culture, bible knowledge, heritage, bank balance, qualifications, post code all play no part in our salvation.

But now in Christ Jesus you who once were far away have been brought near <u>through the blood of Christ.</u>

At the foot of the cross we find fellowship with God, and with one another regardless of class or culture, regardless of the colour of our skin or the size of our bank balance, or the length of our list of good works.

Through the blood of Christ, the purifying sacrificial death of Christ, we are brought near to God, and near to one another.

"Christ himself is our peace, who has made the two one and has destroyed the barrier, the dividing wall of hostility."

Once upon a time there was a wall. A big, high wall. A wide, hollow wall. An ugly, wobbly wall.

It had been built between two bungalows by two men who didn't know much about building, Mr Chalk and Mr Cheese. They'd built it because they hated being neighbours. And they hated being neighbours because they were so completely different. Mr Chalk was a retired teacher - he loved reading his books; he enjoyed playing the violin and he enjoyed doing crosswords. Mr Cheese was a retired chef - a fun-lover, who enjoyed trying new recipes and throwing parties.

"Him and his noisy friends. They keep me awake until midnight," Mr Chalk would moan.
"Him and that awful violin. He wakes me up at six in the morning," Mr Cheese would groan.

The only thing these gentlemen shared was a love of cats. Since moving in, Mr Chalk had taken in a stray cat called Wordsworth, and Mr Cheese had been adopted by a cat called Kippers.

Wordsworth slept most of the time and ate very little, while Kippers pounced on shadows, swung on the curtains and ate everything in sight. In other words, they seemed as different as their owners.

And then one day both cats went missing.

Mr Chalk realised that Wordsworth had gone first thing in the morning, when the animal wasn't curled up in his usual spot.

Mr Cheese realised that Kippers had gone later in the day, when the cat didn't appear for lunch.

That afternoon both men headed off in different directions into the countryside to search for their pets. Mr Chalk kept calling for Wordsworth; Mr Cheese called out for Kippers. But it was no good. After a whole afternoon of calling and searching, both men came home empty-handed.

For once they actually spoke to each other. "You

didn't happen to you see a quiet, sensible cat called Wordsworth while you were out, did you?" asked Mr Chalk. "No," said Mr Cheese. "Did you see a noisy, crazy cat called Kippers?" "No," growled Mr Chalk. "And I hope your cat hasn't led mine into mischief."

"Not a chance of it," said Mr Cheese. "Your cat is too sad and boring. My Kippers wouldn't have anything to do with him." "How dare you!" shouted Mr Chalk. "My Wordsworth is extremely well bred - not at all the sort of cat to mix with your Kippers."

Just as things were turning nasty, a desperate sound filled the air. It was the sound of a cat miaowing. Both men spun round. To their surprise the sound seemed to be coming from inside the wall.

Mr Chalk fetched a ladder and climbed up and examined the wall. And he found a big hole in the stonework.

"There's a hole," he shouted down to Mr Cheese. "Our cats must have fallen through."

Even as he spoke, the cats stopped miaowing and started to thump about.

"They're panicking," cried Mr Chalk. "Or fighting," said Mr Cheese.

The thumping got worse. In fact it sounded as if elephants, not cats, were throwing their bodies against the wall. Before long, cracks had appeared.

Mr Chalk hurried down the ladder. No sooner had he reached the ground than... the wall collapsed with a great CRASH! As the dust settled, a marmalade-coloured cat stepped out from the rubble, safe and sound.

"It's Wordsworth!" cried Mr Chalk.
"No, it isn't! It's Kippers!" cried Mr Cheese.
"No, it isn't - it's Wordsworth," repeated Mr Chalk.
"It's Kippers," insisted Mr Cheese.

The cat rubbed round their ankles. And then the penny dropped. Kippers and Wordsworth were the same cat.

Shaking their heads in amazement, the cat's joint owners sat down side by side on the ruins and they tried to work out how they'd managed to share the same pet for all this time without knowing it.

"No wonder he wasn't hungry when he came to me in the mornings, said Mr Chalk.
"No wonder he was ready to eat and play when he came to me in the afternoons," said Mr Cheese.

They talked on, and do you know what? Mr Cheese didn't find Mr Chalk boring at all, while Mr Chalk was pleasantly surprised to discover how much Mr Cheese knew.

At their feet a purring cat washed his whiskers. It had been hard work bringing that wall down!

Knocking down walls is, indeed, hard work, but as far as we are concerned, Christ has done all the hard work. In him the barriers are down, and if we insist on continuing to rebuild them, or to maintain the walls, especially between believers, then we are guilty of the sin of disobedience. We are guilty of hindering God's plans and purposes for all of us, his purpose being to build not a dividing wall, but *a holy temple.*

In him - in Christ - the whole building is joined together and rises to become a <u>holy temple</u> in the Lord. And in him you too (Jew and Gentile) are being built together to become a dwelling in which God lives by his Spirit.

Prayer

Lord, bring us back to the foot of the cross, and help us first of all to look up and to be reminded of the real cost of our salvation - the blood of Christ, his suffering and death upon the cross.

And then as we kneel there, help us to look around us and to see that we are not alone, that our need of forgiveness and peace and salvation is shared by others, that we are not better than they are, and they are no better than we are.

But now in Christ Jesus WE who once were far away have been brought near through the blood of Christ... near to you, Lord, and near to one another.

Lord, help us then to rise from our knees and stand together as your children, pardoned, delivered, at peace with you and with one another, united, our lives bound together with and in Christ, in whose name we pray. Amen

EPHESIANS
3:1-13

There was this man who loved mystery dramas, so he went to the theatre one evening, which happened to be the opening night of a new murder mystery play. The problem was that his seat was a long way from the stage.

He called an usher over and whispered, "I just love a good mystery, and I have been eagerly waiting for the opening of this play. But I like to follow all the clues very carefully so that I can enjoy the play to the full. I really need to be closer to the stage. If you can get me a better seat, I'll make sure you'll be rewarded."

The usher nodded and said he would be back in a few moments. Thinking he was in for a large tip, the usher spoke with the girl in the box office, hoping to find a better seat for the man.

Just three minutes before the curtain was due to rise, an uncollected ticket became available, so he grabbed it and went to the man and whispered "Follow me."

The usher led the man down to the second row, and

proudly pointed to an empty seat right in the middle. There couldn't have been a better seat.

"Thank you so much," said the man, "This seat is perfect." And then he handed the usher 50p.

The usher looked down at the coin, and with a look of disappointment on his face, leaned over and whispered, "The butler did it in the sitting room with the candlestick."

We love a good mystery, don't we, especially when the answer comes at the appropriate time. I suppose part of the appeal is trying to work out "whodunnit" or at the very least *guess* "whodunnit", opting for the least likely looking person, or if there is a guest actor, that person is likely to be the killer!

Paul is about to reveal a mystery to the believers at Ephesus, but his readers, and indeed even Paul himself in his earlier life as a fanatical Jew, would never have guessed the truth at the heart of the mystery of the gospel, let alone have worked it out.

We are going to see if we can work out what this mystery is (and it isn't too difficult). And then we will consider the role of the Church in sharing this mystery. After that we will think about what Paul says is a consequence of this mystery.

First a brief word about Paul's situation. Paul describes himself as being "**the prisoner of Christ Jesus**". Notice that - he never sees himself as a prisoner of the emperor, does he? Or of the Jews. Or the local authorities. He is always a prisoner of Christ Jesus.

The Jews have accused Paul of treason against the emperor, and now Paul is in Rome awaiting trial by Nero. He is under the watchful eye of the palace guard. And yet he never says he's Caesar's prisoner, does he? This is because he knows Jesus has the last word regarding what happens to him.

What a lesson for all of us - that Jesus has the last word regarding what happens to us in life.

Paul believed it was Christ who determined how long he would remain a prisoner - Christ and not Caesar and therefore he was Christ's prisoner.

The reason for his imprisonment is given as being "*for the sake of you Gentiles*". He's been preaching the gospel of God's grace to the Gentiles - non-Jews - which, of course was unacceptable to the Jews themselves, hence their hostility, opposition.

So much for verse 1, which is incomplete. Paul is suddenly distracted and doesn't get back on track until v 14! And the focus of what follows is this mystery that he speaks about - this "*mystery made known to me*".

What is this mystery then? It centres on Christ and the unsearchable, unfathomable, inestimable riches of Christ, and that through Christ living in us and we in him, all believers - both Jew and

Gentile - are heirs *together* and members *together* of one body and sharers (or partakers) *together* in the promise in Christ Jesus.

Heady stuff, isn't it? The key word there "*together*". This will have been exciting for the Gentiles and unacceptable to the Jews, this idea of Jew and Gentile believers standing together as one, equal under the banner of Christ crucified, sharing together these unsearchable riches of Christ which include the riches of his love for us, the riches of his grace and mercy towards us, the riches of his presence at all times, and his power, and his purposes. The riches of the privilege of being central to God's plans (but more of that when we look at the role of the Church).

The mystery is this tremendous truth that the Gentiles are fellow heirs, members of the same body, sharers in the promise in Christ Jesus. We are all one in Christ.

Jews will have found this a bitter pill to swallow. And indeed we may pay lip service to this truth and yet sometimes behave at least as if some Christians are more equal than others!

The fact is - whether they're serious, sombre and seemingless graceless folk or exuberant and insensitive enthusiasts - we are all equal, we are all heirs *together* and members *together* of one body and sharers (or partakers) *together* in the promise in Christ Jesus

I like an illustration I came across in my preparation this week. During the American civil war two Union army officers climbed a hill in northern Virginia overlooking a Confederate camp.

They had heard about the fierce fighting in the area and were now getting their first glance at the enemy.

As they looked through their telescopes, they saw men lounging about in shirt sleeves, some of them smoking their pipes and washing their clothes, others kicking a ball.

Eventually the officers put down their telescopes and looked at each other amazed, "Wow! they're human beings just like us!"

The Jews needed to realise this. That the Gentiles were human beings just like them, and that before God and in Christ they were equals, sharing together in the promise in Christ.

What does that mean? *"the promise in Christ Jesus."*

Some say it means salvation, others, the gift of the Holy Spirit. I think it's both since salvation is more than just forgiveness of sins and peace with God. It includes the gift of the Holy Spirit to empower us, enable us to be and to do everything God wants us to be and to do.

It's God's will that we - the body of Christ - should deny ourselves, lay down our lives and do things that are not only hard to do but impossible without the enabling power of God.

In the context of the local Church we are called to live in community with each other, called to set aside personal, individual preferences in favour, not of the majority but in favour of God's will.

We are called to respect one another, and forgive one another, and serve one another, and support and encourage one another. And all this is impossible without God's power working in us.

As Paul continues, we find that the Church has a very important role to play regarding all this.

The Church is not a building,
the Church is not a steeple,
the Church is not a resting place,
*the Church is – **people**.*

The Church is people who love Christ, who give their lives to him, who want to follow Jesus, obeying his commands and trusting him to forgive and help us.

This means that we *together* (not individuals but together in unity and fellowship) have a central role in God's plans. And this in turn means that the Church is important to God, and ought therefore to be important to us.

Sadly nowadays there seems to be a lack of understanding of some of the great doctrines, teachings of the Bible. And the irony is that in the Church there is little understanding of the nature and purpose of the Church.

Most of us appreciate the fact that the Church isn't the building and furnishings and so on, but for many of us this is as far as it goes.

To say the Church is people isn't enough. Otherwise the Church can become no more than a club or society, a sort of spiritual BUPA, a social institution existing mainly for the benefit of its members.

This is not what the Bible says about the Church. The Church is a community, a fellowship of believers gathered together by God, living under the headship of Christ, and committed to doing his will. The Church is central to God's purposes and activity in the today's world, as well as being part of his larger purpose – as Paul puts it – *in the heavenly realms.*

v 10 - *His intent was that now, <u>through the Church,</u> the manifold wisdom of God should be made known to the rulers and authorities in the heavenly realms, according to his eternal purpose which he accomplished in Christ Jesus our Lord.*

Do you realise that it's us Paul's is speaking about? But what is he actually saying? He is saying that we are called to be the means of teaching, showing, making known the *manifold wisdom of God to the rulers and authorities in the heavenly realms.*

That word "*manifold*" means "*multi-coloured*" in the Greek.

One way of understanding this is that God's wisdom is able to deal with all shades of life and human experience – golden days and dark days. And our task is to demonstrate to the heavenly beings something of the grace and mercy of God in all the circumstances of life.

The Bible is quite clear in stating that we are surrounded by an invisible spiritual kingdom made up of both good and evil spiritual beings - angels and demons. That's why - in Eph 6 for example - Paul says... *our struggle is not against flesh and blood, but against the rulers, against the authorities, against the powers of this dark world and against the spiritual forces of evil in the heavenly realms.*

If such forces don't exist, then it doesn't make much sense to speak of spiritual warfare and the need for armour.

Angels are at a disadvantage compared with us. They just can't understand God's love. They can only understand his holiness, whereas we have experienced God's love even if we struggle with understanding his holiness.

As they see this love demonstrated in our lives and in the life of the Church, the angels' praise begins to ring out in amazement and wonder at God -- the God of justice, the God of infinite holiness whom they know . They discover that this God is also able to find a way by which he can lavish his love upon those who deserve the full extent of God's wrath.

As one writer - W A Criswell - puts it… *What an exalted conception and idea of the Church this is! What the angelic beings did not learn in the presence of Deity, and what they have not learned in all the providences of God through the centuries, they learn in how God saves man, and in how God's redemptive grace is building this new creation, the Church, the body of the Lord.*

The Church is not a game. It isn't a quaint, old-fashioned pastime. When we get caught up in petty squabbles and trivial pursuits and behave like spoilt children, perhaps we ought to turn to this passage and remind ourselves that the angels are watching us and hoping to learn something about God's nature from what they see in us.

We have then looked at the mystery, which really means something hidden, God's secret revealed at the appropriate time, this tremendous truth that both Jews and Gentiles have a new identity as we stand together as equals under the banner of Christ's cross.

And we have looked at the role of the Church in all this, in teaching heavenly beings a thing or two.

But we can't leave this passage without touching on v 12 *In him (in Christ Jesus) and through faith in him we may approach God with freedom and confidence.*

It is a simple sentence. Something we may even take for granted. But it is a great truth nonetheless.

When, some time ago, – I decided I needed to see a doctor for the first time in a good few years – probably more than ten years! – I didn't want to see him in two, three or four days time. I wanted to see him as soon as possible. That's the way it usually is if we are not feeling well and decide we need to see our doctor, isn't it? But it isn't always possible. *(At the time of editing these sermons for publication, "weeks" should perhaps be substituted there for "days"!)*

What Paul is saying is this - that God's door is open right now, even as I speak. He is available right now. Through Jesus we have direct access to God at any time and wherever we are.

In him and through faith in him we may approach God with freedom and confidence

I think that freedom and confidence ought to be tempered with a measure of respect and humility in view of who it is we're approaching, but what a wonderful thing to be able to say. That we weak, frail, fumbling, stumbling human creatures have permission to come before such a God and pour out our needs before him, and to find him to be a compassionate, tender, loving father .

Here is another story from the American Civil War. A man was sitting on a park bench in Washington, sitting there crying. His son had deserted his post in battle and was going to face a firing squad very soon. The father had come to try and see President Abraham Lincoln to beg for mercy, but couldn't get past the front gates.

As he sat there, people passed by, but nobody stopped to find out what was wrong, until a little boy came along. He stopped and asked the man why he was crying.

The man poured out his story and ended by saying he believed if he could just talk to the president, his son would be pardoned. The young boy asked the man to follow him.

When they came to the front gate of the White House, the little boy said to the soldiers, "It's all right, he's with me." The man followed in amazement.

They came to the room where President Lincoln was talking with his generals and cabinet members, and guarded by yet another detachment of soldiers.

The young boy pushed inside and jumped up on the president's lap. All talk stopped as the boy said, "Daddy, there's a man I want you to meet. He needs your help."

The man was brought in to talk with the president. And the man's son received the presidential pardon, because the son of the president took an interest in his problem.

I don't know if the story is true, but it offers a good illustration of what God's Son does for us.

I don't need to say any more except repeat *In him and through faith in him we may approach* – not the President of the US –but even better… *we may approach God with freedom and confidence*, and that's something we need to learn to share with others so that they too may find the unsearchable riches of Christ. And so that angels and other spiritual beings may discover even more of the manifold wisdom of the God they serve.

The challenge is for us to commit ourselves to being the Church and fulfilling God's saving purposes in us and through us.

EPHESIANS
3: 14-21

Verses 20,21- **Now to him who is able to do immeasurably more than all we ask or imagine, according to his power that is at work within us, to him be glory in the church and in Christ Jesus throughout all generations, for ever and ever!**

God is able to do infinitely more than we can ever think to ask of him or ever imagine he could do! But do you really believe that? Do you think that we as Christians have really got hold of this truth, that God is able to do infinitely more than we can ever think to ask of him or even *imagine* he could do?

These words really ought to inspire, encourage us, even excite us!

One of the dangers of belonging to a larger church, especially one with considerable material resources is the temptation to be self-sufficient and do things in our own strength and using the material resources that we have, and we can easily lose sight of great biblical truths such as this: that **God is able to do infinitely more than we can ever think to ask of him or ever imagine he could do!**

Here in our church we have a mission statement. It is usually printed on the front of the service sheet, and it is also on the wall at the entrance to the church.

We are here to honour the Lord Jesus Christ, to grow in our knowledge and experience of him, and to share his love with each other, our town, nation and world.

When we adopted this as our mission statement a good few years ago, we were saying that we believe that our purpose as a church is first and foremost a missionary purpose - *sharing God's love with each other, our town, nation and world.* And opportunities present themselves to us in a variety of ways here in the town centre, through our position here on one of the main shopping streets, and through our Coffee Shop with its ministry and mission six days a week, as well as opportunities in our daily lives.

But before we can make any real progress in reaching out to people and sharing God's love in words and action, there needs first to be a work of grace, a miracle in our own hearts.

Paul knew this when he was writing to the church at Ephesus. This work of grace was apparently needed there in that church hundreds of years ago.

In the passage before us -Eph 3: 14ff – we find Paul on his knees. Notice that, by the way... **on his knees.** *For this reason I kneel before the Father,*

Paul has just said we can approach God in freedom and confidence, with boldness, but as I said in the previous chapter, this also means with respect and humility. Paul confirms this here. He's on his knees , praying earnestly for this miracle to take place in their lives.

But understand this. Paul isn't praying for miracle of conversion. He was in no doubt whatsoever that they were born again believers. In chapter 1 Paul describes his addressees *as* **the saints in Ephesus, the faithful in Christ Jesus.**

In 1: 13 - *you also were included in Christ when you heard the word of truth, the gospel of your salvation... having believed, you were marked in him with a seal, the promised Holy Spirit...*

They had accepted the gospel. They had received Jesus Christ as Lord and Saviour. This was not in question. But Paul knew that they needed to move on and continue to grow as Christians. They needed to raise their sights and fully grasp the extent of God's love and grace. And so he prays for them.

What does Paul pray?

in v 16 we are told that he prays to God the Father

that *he may strengthen them with power through his Spirit in their inner being.*

"*inner being*" means heart and mind and will - those aspects of our nature that seem to separate us from the rest of creation.

Paul prays for the Holy Spirit to reach the very depths of their inner being. Paul prays this because deep within us is where the Holy Spirit works most effectively, changing our view of the world, changing our response to events, changing our attitudes, our priorities, and giving us a whole new perspective on life.

As Paul's prayer continues, we see what this involves. He prays that this may happen *so that Christ may dwell in your hearts through faith.*

"**dwell**" means "become a permanent resident".

Do you remember that familiar picture in Revelation 3? The risen and ascended Lord Jesus Christ is speaking, and he says, *Behold, I stand at the door and knock. If anyone hears my voice and opens the door, I will come in and eat with him and he with me.*

We usually take this verse and lift it out of its context, don't we? We use it in an evangelistic context as part of the gospel challenge to open that door and let Christ into our lives.

There in Revelation it is not a case of Jesus

standing at the door of the _unbeliever's_ heart, knocking, waiting to be invited in. This is the sad picture of Jesus Christ, the Head of the Church, waiting to be invited back in, trying to gain access to one of the New Testament churches.

The reason is that he is clearly not a permanent resident there in the church at Laodicea. I don't suppose they'd deliberately thrown him out, but somehow, they had managed to exclude Jesus from the life of the church. Why else is he standing on the outside, standing at the door?

Churches can do that today, and when churches do it, it's because the individual Christians who make up the church have pushed Jesus to the edges, the margins of their lives. Consequently Jesus (our Lord and Saviour) becomes a visitor, a guest, when he really wants to be a permanent resident.

Paul prays that the Holy Spirit will work deep within these people so that they are constantly aware of Christ's presence.

Paul prays that they really believe this because if we really believe in the indwelling Christ, it will make a significant difference to the way we live.

Put it this way. If Christ's life is bound up with yours, if he is dwelling in your heart by faith, if he is with you at all times, where have you taken the indwelling Christ in the past 12 months? Or even in the past week? To what experiences did you subject him? Were there places you went to or things you did or said that would embarrass or offend or anger him? Were there programmes on TV you wouldn't have watched if Jesus was there, sitting beside you?

And what about this next week? Will Christ be a permanent resident, or will he find himself standing on the outside from time to time?

Paul prays for this work of grace - that Christ may dwell in our hearts through faith.

He also prays this: (v 17b) *that you, being rooted and established in love, may have the power together with all the saints to grasp how wide and long and high and deep is the love of Christ...*

Notice first of all that Paul is not praying that they should *become* rooted and established in love. Nor is he referring to their love in the sense of love being at the centre of everything they do. Not that it shouldn't be, but this is not what he is saying here.

The tense in Greek indicates that it should read *Having been rooted and established in love...* The love is therefore God's love in Christ Jesus.

The prayer is that *having received* Christ who himself is the expression of God's love, they should be enabled by the Holy Spirit to grasp, to comprehend the immensity, the vastness, the greatness of Christ's love. They should have an overwhelming, awe-inspiring sense of God's love in Christ Jesus.

Paul's prayer is that the Holy Spirit should lead them and us to reflect on all that God has done for our sakes, meditating on the revelation of God's love in his Son Jesus Christ, taking on board the suffering of Christ, the victory of Christ and the grace of the Lord Jesus Christ - *to grasp how wide and long and high and deep is the love of Christ...*

Does your understanding and recognition of God's love in Christ need to be enlarged? The test is found in our own hearts, in the level of genuine and deep compassion and love we have for others.

But having said this, this is all about "conceptual love", understanding with the mind.

If I had the time to do the research, I am sure I could write a whole book on Christ's love, and I would still not *know* the love of Christ. I would still not *grasp* for myself *how wide and long and high and deep is the love of Christ.*

We can study this topic - "the love of Christ" - till the cows come home and still not *know* the love of Christ. That's what I mean by "conceptual love", head knowledge.

So Paul goes on to pray that this conceptual love may become "experiential love".

You see, **to know this love that surpasses**

knowledge is not just about head knowledge, but knowledge grounded in personal experience.

Let me repeat an illustration some of you may have heard before.

Some of you are of the right age to remember a pop singer from the 1960s - Barry McGuire. He sang a protest song called "Eve of Destruction" (when protest songs were all the fashion). He also sang with group a called The New Christy Minstrels whose best-known song was "Four Wheels on my Wagon", but that's beside the point.

Barry McGuire became a Christian and used to go on tour, singing modern gospel songs back in the 1980s. We have an album at home, a live recording of one of his concerts. I have usually found his talk between songs as helpful, if not more helpful than the actual songs!

Once he gave an illustration to help us understand the difference between "conceptual knowledge" and "experiential knowledge" (what he referred to as believers and knowers).

I can't recall the precise details, but it went something like this.

In America they seem to be rather fond of roasting marshmallows, and there's this novice roasting marshmallows for the very first time. He is a complete novice. He has never even seen an open fire before, having been brought up in a high rise flat.

He's roasting a marshmallow on the end of a stick, and being inexperienced, he leaves it there too long. The marshmallow begins to melt and slips off the stick into the fire.

He is just about to reach in when someone says "No. don't do that! You'll burn your fingers!"

He thinks about it, weighs it up for a moment and then nods his head. "That makes sense. I can <u>believe</u> that!". That's conceptual knowledge, head knowledge. He believes what he's been told.

A little while later the same thing happens again, but this new believer does what many new believers do – he slips back into old ways. He's roasting a marshmallow on the end of a stick. He leaves it there too long. The marshmallow begins to melt and slips off the stick into the fire.

He sees the marshmallow there in the ashes and doesn't want to waste it. So he thinks that if he is very quick, it'll be OK.

He plunges his hand into the fire, and feels a sharp, burning sensation, and quickly pulls back again.

He's now moved from <u>conceptual</u> knowledge to <u>experiential</u> knowledge!

Paul prays that Christian believers will not only grasp the immensity of Christ's love but experience it for themselves - *to know this love that surpasses knowledge.*

Paul prays for one more thing, one more way in which this deeper working of the Holy Spirit affects the believer: *that you may be filled to the measure of all the fullness of God.*

What does this mean?

What it does not mean is the way it is translated in the Authorised Version - *filled with the fullness of God.* This would simply be impossible. The whole of creation itself could not accommodate the fullness of God, because God fills the whole universe and beyond. God occupies every bit of space; there is nowhere where God is not.

God is far greater than the sum total of all creation, so there is no way we can be **filled with the fullness of God.**

What it means is this. It means to be filled to capacity with the fullness of God. It's about God completely fulfilling his intentions, his purposes in us. It's about reaching our true potential within his will and purposes.

Well, of course, we may say all this is simply not possible. It's a nice thought, a lovely prayer, but Paul is praying beyond the realms of possibility. How could anyone ever achieve this level of spirituality?

What would Paul say? *God is able to do immeasurably more than all we ask or imagine, according to his power that is at work within us.*

Back in v 16 I skipped over some words.

Paul prays that *out of his glorious riches (God) may strengthen you with power through his Spirit in your inner being.*

"out of his glorious riches" is not really what the Greek says. A better translation is *according to the riches of his glory* . This means - "in proportion to" the riches of his glory, not "out of" his riches. It is a reminder of God's limitless resources.

John Newton captures this in his words...

Thou art coming to a King;
Large petitions with thee bring,
For his grace and power are such,
None can ever ask too much.

Paul is not praying beyond the bounds of possibility. He remembers to whom his prayers are addressed. He believes in a God of inexhaustible riches and incredible power, a God who is able to exceed all expectations. And it's to such a God that Paul prays on behalf of these believers in Ephesus, and it is indeed his prayer for all believers.

But Paul departed this life centuries ago. Who's going to pray this prayer for us now? Well, the

Bible teaches us that Christ himself intercedes on our behalf, as also does the Holy Spirit. But I want to suggest something here.

Paul's prayers give us an insight into his prayer life. This was not necessarily his intention but Paul's prayers are prayers we ourselves can pray. Here is a prayer we can pray for ourselves and for one another.

For example, try this: try re-writing Paul's prayer, making it your own - *that out of his glorious riches God may strengthen* **me** *with power through his Spirit working in my inner being.*

And then try it again with someone else's name in there: *that out of his glorious riches God may strengthen ***** with power through his Spirit working in his/her inner being...*

Or in more general terms, praying for one another: *that out of his glorious riches God may strengthen each of us with power through his Spirit working in our inner being.*

Or you can use it to pray for other churches in this town. There are all kinds of possibilities. And if we commit ourselves to praying in this way, I believe we will begin to see Paul's words coming to life when he says: **to God be the glory in the church and in Christ Jesus, throughout all generations, for ever and ever.** including, of course, this generation, here and now!

EPHESIANS 4:1

*(Each year I would suggest a "Text for the Year" in an attempt to focus our minds on a Bible-based truth or instruction. This sermon relates to the Text for 2005 - **As a prisoner for the Lord, then, I urge you to live a life worthy of the calling you have received.**)*

One day a little 5-year-old boy was playing with his 2-year-old brother when suddenly the 2-year-old reached up and tugged at his older brother's hair.

The older boy screamed in pain, and his mother came rushing in. "He just pulled my hair" said the older boy, tears in his eyes. "Don't make such a fuss - he's only 2 years old and he doesn't know what its like to have his hair pulled," said Mum.

She left the room and seconds later she heard a scream from the bedroom, but this time it was the 2-year-old screaming in pain. She rushed in and asked what had happened. The older brother simply answered, "He knows what it feels like now!"

Of course, the 2 year old did need to learn a lesson, and perhaps the older brother was the one to teach him, but there were lessons for him to learn too.

You see, we can be very good, can't we, at deciding what lessons other people need to learn. Some of us do it on a professional basis while others are mere amateurs but no less dedicated.

You know how it is. We can be sitting in church, listening to the sermon, hopefully, and thinking to ourselves that it's a pity "so-and-so" isn't here listening to this because it's just what he/she needs to hear.

Or if "so-and-so" is here, we may be thinking "I hope "so-and-so" is listening to this and taking note".

We can be very good sometimes at deciding who needs to hear and take note of God's word, but we are not always so good at accepting we ourselves also need to hear and take note.

Our Text for 2005 is this - *As a prisoner for the Lord, then, I urge you to live a life worthy of the calling you have received.*

I believe this is God's word to each and everyone of us, including me, as we begin our journey through 2005, and I believe it's a message we have hardly begun to take seriously.

Paul is urging us to do something most of us have not even thought about doing, and the reason is this. Either we don't know what our calling is, or we don't believe it.

What is this calling Paul has in mind? We are called to be sons and daughters of the God and Father of our Lord Jesus Christ.

Paul, this great apostle, this man of God was an evangelist and teacher. He was always keen to stress that this calling was *all of grace and nothing whatsoever to do with personal merit or status.*

It does not matter how long we have been a Christian. It doesn't matter how long we've been associated with a particular church, or who we are, what position we hold, what achievements we may claim. Were it not for the intervention of Christ at some point in our lives, you and I would be lost forever. Were it not for the seemingly infinite patience and forbearance of God, you and I would be cast out of his presence. Were it not for the grace of God, there would be no spark of goodness in us whatsoever.

So, Paul is keen that we should know that we are privileged sons and daughters of the God and Father of our Lord Jesus Christ. That's who we are. That's our calling, and it's all about grace.

Let me put it this way. We are numbered among the greatest people this world has ever known! We may not feel all that great, but that's who we are. At least, this is what Paul has been saying in the first three chapters of this book.

He says we are blessed, chosen, predestined *(don't worry what that means. Just accept that, if nothing else, it means we were part of God's plans and purposes long before we were even conceived!).*

Paul says we have been adopted as God's children, we have been redeemed, forgiven, filled with the Holy Spirit.

He says we are called to be sons and daughters of the living God, called to display the family likeness, to cause people to say, *"Isn't he just like his father, isn't she just like her father?"*

We are called to reflect God's holiness, to reveal his glory and his greatness, called to allow his character to shine through us.

So, says Paul, start living as sons and daughters of the living God, start living according to who you are. Live a life worthy of your calling, your status, your privileged position.

If you are familiar with the older translations of this verse you will know that word *"live"* in NIV has replaced the word *"walk"*. The Greek word is *peripatesai* from which we get our word *peripatetic"*. The idea is one of movement, and *walk* is a good word instead of *live* because suggests moving forward. Not standing still but making progress, developing.

Paul is not encouraging what's been described as

"*Peter Pan Christianity*". We can't live a life worthy of our calling without growing and developing and maturing.

But notice this before we move on to ask what this means in practice. How does Paul begin this verse?

"*As a prisoner for the Lord...*"

This is a reminder that this **walk** will not always lead to green pastures.

Paul was a prisoner of Rome, chained to a Roman soldier day and night. This was the result of his uncompromising faithfulness to his Lord.

Here then is our Text for 2005 *As a prisoner for the Lord, then, I urge you to live a life worthy of the calling you have received.*

But what does this mean in practice? It's alright in theory but what does it mean in practice?

Paul wastes no time spelling it out for us. Verse 2 *Be completely humble and gentle.*

Notice that short word "*be*". *Be completely humble and gentle.*

It isn't so much about what we do in the first place but about what (or who) we are. Who we are determines what we do, not other way round. It isn't what we do that determines who we are. This is the wrong way round if we are going to *live a life worthy of the calling we have received.*

Be completely humble and gentle. This is about genuine humility, not an act, a pretence of false humility. This is not the nauseating, nasty, Uriah Heep type of false self-denigration, not the kind of humility that draws attention to oneself. This isn't humility at all; it's attention seeking.

Paul here is referring to genuine humility. And as for *be gentle* - the word is usually translated "*meek*".

Translators seem to avoid that word these days, probably because meekness tends to be equated with weakness. Actually it is quite the opposite. Meekness is about power and strength, but it's power and strength under control.

An old commentary that I have makes this observation: *There is not one of us who needs among his Christian brethren to take care of his dignity - God and men will take care of that. What is necessary is to take care of lowliness and meekness.*

Be completely humble and gentle.

In other words, follow the example of Christ, walk the way of Christ, even if it also means the way of the cross.

And *be patient* - slow to anger, slow to take offence. Make a real attempt at understanding the other person rather than losing your temper and self-control. As it has been said, "*every fit of anger* *against another wounds <u>us</u> and not him".* Or as someone else put it, *"anger burns up the soul that contains it".*

Noel Brooks, in his exposition of this passage, writes: *In the church of Christ, especially in local churches, where Christians have to worship and work closely together, there is ample opportunity for the exercise of patience.*

Paul also urges tolerance - **bearing with one another in love.** Regarding this, another writer says this: *The Church is not a society for the perfect; it's a hospital for those who are being made whole under Jesus the Great Physician.*

"not a society for the perfect" - we understand this concerning ourselves, but can at times expect perfection in everyone else!

The Christians at Ephesus were far from perfect, as were the Christians at Corinth, Galatia, and most of other New Testament churches. Even the disciples themselves were far from perfect. And so are we!

So, Paul says... **As a prisoner for the Lord, then, I urge you to live a life worthy of the calling you have received.**

What does this mean in practice? It means **Be completely humble, and gentle; be patient, bearing with one another in love.**

In other words, says Paul, in v 3 - *Make every effort to keep the unity of the Spirit through the bond of peace.*

Notice that this "*unity of the Spirit*" is God's gift to us. We can't create or manufacture it, and we are not expected to. But we are expected to make every effort, to work hard, at maintaining and protecting, guarding this unity.

"*make every effort*" is a very strong expression. It means much more than not doing anything to damage our unity. Of course, it means that in the first place. And there are various ways in which we can threaten or damage or compromise our unity, harmony, peace.

But Paul is saying: "be eager, make every effort to guard this unity, to protect it, to repair it where it is broken, to strengthen it where it is weak."

We may have done nothing to disturb the peace and fellowship of the church, but we may also have done nothing to foster, or cultivate or strength our unity as God's people.

"*make every effort*" - *work at thinking the best of one another, saying the best to one another and speaking the best about one another.*

Here we stand at the beginning of a New Year with all its possibilities and opportunities. A year in which God can and will do some amazing things, both in us and through us.

If you find that hard to believe, then I suggest you look again at Eph 3:20

What does Paul say... *Now to him who is able to do immeasurably more than all we ask or imagine, according to his power that is at work within us, to him be glory in the church and in Christ Jesus throughout all generations, for ever and ever!* *beginning here and now in the year 2005.*

But perhaps we need to track back even further to Eph 3:16 and read again Paul's prayer, and commit ourselves to praying this prayer for one another, not just in a general sense but one or two individuals - the people who sit near us in church, or people we meet in our house groups or through other church activities, or on our deacons lists:

I pray that out of his glorious riches God may strengthen you with power through his Spirit in your inner being, so that Christ may dwell in your hearts through faith. And I pray that you, being rooted and established in love, may have power, together with all the saints, to grasp how wide and long and high and deep is the love of Christ, and to know this love that surpasses knowledge--that you may be filled to the measure of all the fullness of God.

Why not pray this prayer for one or two individuals each day, and in this way help them also to make progress in *living a life worthy of the calling they have received.*

EPHESIANS 4:1-16

Many years ago, when I was a child, one of the things we used to do as a family was to go to the Ideal Home exhibition - not the one in London but we used to have one in Nottingham, at the Ice Stadium. I used to enjoy it, mainly because we could collect lots of leaflets and sometimes free samples.

Of course, people's idea of an ideal home has changed over the years, and if we were to look back on some of the photographs and adverts from the 1950s, I am sure we would find them quite amusing nowadays. The latest, very modern, contemporary designs then would now have a very dated look.

There is, apparently, no single design of house, together with interior decoration, furniture and furnishings and equipment that constitutes the ideal home. Why? You would have thought that after all these years we might have arrived at something constituting an ideal home, but fashion changes over the years, and tastes change.

We only have to think of the colours of bathroom suites 20-25 years ago and the fact that the only acceptable colour nowadays is white, it seems! And whereas we used to cover up a multitude of sins with Artex – textured paint - and woodchip wallpaper, these are not at all trendy these days.

So, there really is no such thing as an "ideal home". But what about churches? Is there such a thing as an ideal church? Not a *perfect* church but an *ideal* church. And what comes to mind when we think of an ideal church?

Some might think of a certain type of building with stunning architecture, interior décor, lots of useful meeting rooms, and nowadays, the latest hi-tech equipment for sound and vision, and even lighting.

Others might think more in terms of services and liturgy and music. And others may judge a church by its programme of activities, youth work, the importance of outreach and social action.

Some may even see the ideal church as a mixture of all of these features.

In Ephesians 4 Paul gives his picture of an ideal church, and he says nothing about buildings, although it helps if we have somewhere to meet!

He says nothing about music, although he does

encourage singing praises to God using a variety of musical styles.

He says nothing about a programme of activities, although some of these may serve the aims and purpose of the church.

What is Paul's picture of an ideal church? It is one where each person has a ministry, each person plays his or her part in ensuring that the whole church functions as God intends.

When we think of "ministers" what do we think of? At one time the word "minister" might have conjured up a picture of a person in a dark suit, or an academic gown, or a cassock, and, of course, the essential and collar turned the wrong way round!

Ministers – in that sense – are not so easily identified these days but when we think of a minister, we still tend to think of what we call ordained ministry. We think of those who are called and have been trained at a bible college or theological college, and whose call has been examined and tested in the wider church beyond their own local church.

In other words, we tend to think of "professional", paid ministry. We might possibly stretch it to a lay ministry - someone who has undergone little or no formal training perhaps, and no formal testing of their vocation - but we are generally inclined to see ministry as the province of one person

(or in a larger church, perhaps two or even more recognised leaders.)

I don't know when this concept began, but somewhere in church history we developed this demarcation line between what we call "clergy" and "laity"- those who *do* ministry, offer ministry, and those who *receive* it.

This is not the Biblical model of either ministry or the church. As one writer puts it – *the real need is to eliminate the laity!* And just in case there is any possibility of misunderstanding what he means, he is saying that we need to get rid of the <u>concept</u> of a laity by equipping everyone to be ministers.

To understand ministry in terms of one or two specific people within a local church is to have a limited and disabling view of ministry.

It is limited for a very simple reason. Biblically speaking ministry is something to which ALL Christians are called without exception.

Notice that... to which all **are** called, not to which all **may be** called.

Look at Ephesians 4: the second part of v 1 *live a life worthy of the calling <u>you</u> have received.*

Paul was addressing all the believers at Ephesus.

In v 12 he refers to <u>all</u> God's people being prepared for *works of service so that the whole body of Christ may be built up.*

v 16 – makes it clear that each part of the body of the Christ has its work to do.

From him the whole body, joined and held together by every supporting ligament, grows and builds itself up in love, as each part does its work.

Every believer, every member of the church is a minister because the word means, quite simply "*one who serves*". To confine our understanding of ministry to what we call "the ordained ministry" is to limit the New Testament meaning of this word "*ministry*".

It is also disabling because it throws the weight of responsibility on to the shoulders of just one (or 2) people who are expected to have a whole galaxy of gifts, and a huge amount of time in which to exercise those gifts, compared with the rest of the church membership!

It can't be done, and so this view has a disabling effect on the church because the church operates less effectively than it could.

Paul says - (v 7) *to each one of us grace has been given as Christ apportioned it.* Here grace means a gift - *to each one of us a gift has been given as Christ apportioned it.*

This is made clear in the verse that follows...

v 8 quoting Psalm 68 – ***When he ascended on high, he led captives in his train and gave gifts to men.***

Grace is, of course, something we do not deserve, but did you notice? He says **to each one of us.** No one has all the gifts, but everyone has some gift or other entrusted to him or her for the benefit of the church.

Various gifts are mentioned in the New Testament. Paul is about to mention some here but let's save that for a few moments.

It's important to understand this. The gifts he's about to list are not all the gifts God gives. There are several   lists in the New Testament and at least 20 specific gifts are named, including things like "serving" and "showing mercy", encouraging, contributing to the needs of others. And even then I am sure God's list of gifts has not been exhausted.

What is a gift? It has been defined as *a heightened ability.* For example, we can all communicate and instruct and teach to some degree or other, sometimes without even realising it, but some have a *heightened ability* to communicate or teach.

We can all pray but some have a *heightened ability* to pray.

We can all reach out in love to care for somebody, but some have a *heightened ability* to care for others.

A gift is a *heightened ability* .

It's important to understand something else as well. The gifts God gives are not abstract, disembodied talents and abilities. They are given to people in a particular context and for a particular purpose. Gifts are also given to individuals but given for the benefit of the church, not for that individual person's benefit, and certainly not for that person's status or prestige.

What all this means is this. The real gifts God gives to his church are *people*! God gives people in whom he has placed his gifts.

Incredible though this may sound, you – whoever you are – are God's gift to this church!

Without you and whatever heightened ability God has given you, this church is incomplete and not able to fulfil its God-given purpose.

You are a vital part of the body of Christ. You, whoever you are, are essential for the church's life, health and wellbeing.

Paul goes on to mention some of the *people-gifts* God gives to the church...

v 11 **It was he who gave some to be apostles, some to be prophets, some to be evangelists, and some to be pastors and teachers**

These are what we call "leadership gifts". Each

member has a ministry, an area of service within the life of the church, and one particular area of service is leadership. But let's get one thing straight. Church leaders are not more important than anyone else in the church. It's just that they have gifts, heightened abilities that can be used in leading God's people, and by their nature these tend to be high profile gifts.

Some people are "born leaders", natural leaders. There is something about them, their manner, their self-confidence that enables them to lead others.

Imagine you are in a church hall and chairs are scattered all over the place. Imagine you are in a group of, say, 10 people in there, and someone asks the group to move the chairs so that they all face the same direction, but gives no specific guidance.

What is likely to happen? Someone will emerge as a leader and take the initiative and get things moving.

In any group of people, some sort of leadership will emerge, but a natural leader isn't always the best person to achieve the required results.

They might get the chairs all facing one way, but it could be the wrong way. Or a natural leader may also be naturally cautious when courage and vision are called for, or the other way round - courageous and visionary when a measure of caution is needed.

In Christian leadership, knowledge and insight and understanding and vision are what's needed, and only God can supply these. These heightened abilities are given by God.

Notice also that Paul says... *he who gave <u>some</u> to be apostles, <u>some</u> to be prophets, <u>some</u> to be evangelists, and <u>some</u> to be pastors and teachers.*

He seems to roll pastors and teachers into one *(probably because one of tasks of a pastor, shepherd is to feed the sheep, and teaching is about feeding with the word of God).*

Apart from bringing those two together, pastors and teachers, Paul separates the other areas of leadership. He doesn't expect all these gifts to be found in one person.

Why does God give these leadership gifts. Paul states very clearly why God gives such leaders to the church.
v 12 *to prepare God's people for works of service, so that the body of Christ may be built up* - i.e. to train and equip God's people for ministry!

Leaders are not meant to do all the works of service, but to prepare God's people to minister.

Leadership then is just one ministry among many within the church, where every member is a minister, and every minister is a servant.

And the aim is that ***the body of Christ may be built up until we all reach unity in the faith and in the knowledge of the Son of God and become mature, attaining to the whole measure of the fullness of Christ.***

There are various kinds of unity. A brick wall is a picture of one kind of unity, involving uniformity, where every brick is the same. A car engine is a picture of a different kind of unity, made of many different parts, different materials, different functions, all working with one overall purpose - to provide power.

The New Testament picture of unity is the human body, made up of different parts, different materials, different functions, all working together.

If we get it right, Paul says we will be both *protecting* the church and *building* the church.

Protecting the church: v 14 - ***Then we will no longer be infants, tossed back and forth by the waves, and blown here and there by every wind of teaching and by the cunning and craftiness of men in their deceitful scheming.***

Building the church: v 16 ***From him (Christ) the whole body, joined and held together by every supporting ligament, grows and builds itself up in love, as each part does its work.***

Back in vv 1 and 2 Paul says: *I urge you to live a life worthy of the calling you have received. Be completely humble and gentle; be patient, bearing with one another in love.*

We are called to be servants just as Christ came *not to be served but to serve.*

Paul reminds us of the characteristics every servant needs, based on the example of Christ himself.

be completely humble i.e. recognising the value of other people and the needs of other people.

be completely gentle i.e. meekness - but not weakness. Meekness means not asserting our rights.

and be patient, bearing with one another.

I like what Noel Brooks writes in his exposition of this passage (quoted also in the previous chapter!)...

In the church of Christ, especially in local churches, where Christians have to worship and work closely together, there is ample opportunity for the exercise of patience.

All this is so that the body of Christ can function properly, with all its parts working together and not against each other.

What then is an ideal church? Not a church with great architecture and interior design. Not a church with your type of music, whatever that may be. And not a church with a full and balanced programme of activities.

An ideal church is a church where the leadership focuses on feeding and equipping God's people, and where the members understand and accept that they also are ministers - everyone of them!

EPHESIANS
4:17 – 5:2

Conventional wisdom is part of everyday life. What do I mean by this? I am referring to those catchy sayings that we sometimes use to guide us in life.

"Give him an inch and he'll take a mile" we may say, and so we apply a bit of caution.

"Two wrongs don't make a right."
"God helps those that help themselves".

Here's one I like (and I expect apostle Paul would have liked it too) - *"If you lie down with dogs you'll get up with fleas."*

And how about this well-known saying? *"When in Rome do as the Romans do."*

All this is "conventional wisdom", and sometimes it's helpful. But not always. For example - I don't think *"God helps those that help themselves"* is really a gospel principle. And I'm not sure about *"When in Rome do as the Romans do."*

On the surface this may seem like a reasonable and sensible thing to do, adapting to the culture we find ourselves in. In 1 Corinthians 9 Paul himself writes *I have become all things to all people.*

He had adapted himself according to the circumstances and the people he was with, and so he says - *to the Jews I became like a Jew …To those under the law I became like one under the law … to those not having the law I became like one not having the law …*
to the weak I became weak…

This wasn't about blending in just for the sake of it though. There was a purpose in Paul's policy. He said - *I have become all things to all people so <u>that by all possible means I might save some</u>. I do all this for the sake of the gospel.*

He would have been horrified at the thought of *"When in Rome do as the Romans do."*

Wherever we find ourselves, our first priority above all else is to adopt a lifestyle that honours God and includes God, and so Paul says… *I tell you this, and insist on it in the Lord, that you must no longer live as the Gentiles do.*

"When in Rome do NOT do as the Romans do!"

And then Paul begins to paint a grim picture of what he means.

Of course, when he says "Gentiles" Paul means those who do not worship the one true God. He does not mean all non-Jews because strictly speaking that would include Christian believers as well.

For the Jew the world was divided into two classes of people - Jew and Gentile, but for Paul it seems there are three classes of people - Jew, Gentile and Christian believer. And to believers Paul says - *you must no longer live as the Gentiles do.*

He goes on to describe them in terms of *the futility of their thinking, their darkened understanding, their alienation from God, their ignorance, their hardened hearts, their insensitivity, and their insatiable hunger for every kind of impurity.*

What he's saying is that all their thinking, their philosophies, their intellect, their knowledge, are all futile, empty and meaningless and ultimately are worthless because they leave out the most important part.

They're darkened in their understanding. The word used here for "understanding" is a combination of two words which mean "applied knowledge".

Paul says they are stumbling round in the dark, alienated from God because of their ignorance.

"Ignorance" is a key word here. I understand as

meaning that they have ignored God and therefore know nothing about him or what he expects of us. It was the result of either neglect or a deliberate decision to leave God out of their lives, or exclude him from part of their lives.

There was and is a widespread ignorance as far as God is concerned. It is ironic that in our world where science and technology have accomplished some remarkable things, including landing man on the moon, and sending space probes even further, transmitting signals back to earth – it is ironic in a world where we can be overwhelmed with information through the media of TV and radio and books and the internet, that where it really matters, there is a widespread ignorance concerning our Creator.

There is a widespread disregard for God, a failure, in our quest for knowledge, to recognise God's place in the scheme of things.

And despite uncovering and discovering a lot of truth about the universe and life in general, worldly thinking is doomed and futile and meaningless if it chooses to ignore God.

It is doomed because if God is not part of the picture, we have no accountability beyond ourselves, no relationship with God, no desire to honour and serve God.

We become accountable only to ourselves, serving

only our own interests, and the result is seen in v 19 - *Having lost all sensitivity, they have given themselves over to sensuality so as to indulge in every kind of impurity, with a continual lust for more.*

Paul is saying that the basic problem that leads to sin is flawed thinking in the first place. It begins in the mind. So Paul continues: *you must no longer live as the Gentiles do, in the futility of their thinking.*

As believers, we must think differently, or as we say today, we must adopt a different mindset.

The question is "How?" How do we do this?

The answer is found in vv 22-24 - *You were taught, with regard to your former way of life, to put off your old self, which is being corrupted by its deceitful desires; to be made new in the attitude of your minds; and to put on the new self, created to be like God in true righteousness and holiness.*

I am reminded of Romans 12 where Paul writes: *Do not conform any longer to the pattern of this world, but be transformed by the renewing of your mind.*

The picture Paul creates here is one of taking off our old clothes or getting rid of our old clothes.

I spent some time doing this a few days ago. The Salvation Army were in the area collecting unwanted clothing, and I decided it was time to give up any hope of ever having a 38" waist again or anything close to that! And I didn't need all those jogging bottoms and polo shirts since, sadly, I don't play football anymore! And some shirts had seen better days, and some had seen smaller neck sizes, and some had seen the washing machine too often and had faded. The bottom line is that I filled two large black bags with unwanted clothing!

But notice that I *decided* to do all this. The old, unwanted clothes didn't jump into the bags of their own accord. It took a deliberate decision on my part. Several deliberate decisions, in fact.

It's the same with getting rid of the old self. It doesn't just happen. Paul says **with regard to your former way of life, _put off_ your old self, which is being corrupted by its deceitful desires.**

That's a general principle, and he will go on to give some detail in the verses that follow, but he's talking about getting rid of the old clothes, the old self, the old life characterised, corrupted by *"deceitful desires".*

These desires include sexual immorality (which Paul mentions in 5:3), but it can include other desires as well.

For example, the urge to spend and acquire possessions (known as "retail therapy" these days). Such an urge can be deceitful because we never find satisfaction in owning things. We always hunger for more.

Some people realise this, so they don't go collecting things. They collect experiences instead and again; these don't really satisfy either. And so nowadays we have <u>extreme</u> sports and activities.

Some people hunger for power, whether over whole nations or just over one or two people. This can lead to corruption, building up our own ego at the expense of other people's, and in its commonest form, bullying. None of this will ever satisfy.

The urge to criticise other people, or to wallow in self-pity, or to be a martyr, or to oppose those who don't think or act as we do, or to be "holier-than-thou" - all of these are deceitful desires.

Deceitful desires have this one thing in common – self! They have self at the centre, self as the focus of life, the centre of attention.

Paul says we're to get rid of these old clothes.
Therefore each of you must put off falsehood.

And then ***In your anger do not sin*** – learn the difference between righteous anger and wrong anger.

He who has been stealing must steal no longer.

Do not let any unwholesome talk come out of your mouths - this includes discouraging words, gossip, destructive criticism and so on.

Get rid of all bitterness, rage and anger, brawling and slander, along with every form of malice.

And in 5:3 – get rid of sexual immorality, any impurity, greed, obscenity, coarse joking etc.

All of these are the old clothes we need to dispose of.

Now, when I'd filled my two black bags full of unwanted clothes, I ended up with a half empty wardrobe, empty shelves and drawers and lots of storage space, which was fine. But it is not good to leave empty space when we get rid of the old life, the old self.

So Paul also says - *put off your old self... and put on the new self, created to be like God in true righteousness and holiness.*

Leave the old self, the old attitudes and values and vices where they belong – in the past - and put on the new clothes God provides.

You see, when we believe in Jesus Christ and accept him as our Lord and Saviour, we are given a new nature - a nature that is able to live in God's way.

This is something the old nature just can't do. No matter how dissatisfied a person may feel, no matter how much we may realise there's something wrong and we need to change, we can't do it without the new clothes, the new nature God provides in Christ. We need to put the new clothes on, having first removed the old ones.

Again Paul gives some examples of what he means.

You must put off falsehood and speak truthfully to your neighbour.

Stop stealing and work, *doing something useful with your own hands, that you may have something to share with those in need.*

Do not let any unwholesome talk come out of your mouths, **but** *only what is helpful for building others up according to their needs*,

and **Get rid of all bitterness, rage and anger, brawling and slander, along with every form of malice. Be kind and compassionate to one another, forgiving each other, just as in Christ God forgave you.**

In other words, put on these new clothes which are actually the character of Christ of which compassion and kindness and (in 5:2) love - seem to be key features.

Compassion means a genuine concern for people – for their needs and wellbeing, their hurts and sorrows.

Kindness means compassion in action; it is more than just good intentions and nice thoughts. Kindness is active, practical.

Was Jesus compassionate? He certainly was! Just ask the lepers who he healed, or the blind who were given their sight, or the lame who could walk, or the lonely, the sinners and outcasts. They would all say a resounding "yes!".

But they would only be able to say yes because they had experienced his kindness in tangible ways.

Jesus was, in fact, the expression of God's kindness towards all people, including us. In Ephesians 2:7 Paul writes: *God raised us up with Christ and seated us with him in the heavenly realms in Christ Jesus, in order that in the coming ages he might show the incomparable riches of his grace, <u>expressed in his kindness to us in Christ Jesus.</u>*

Forgiveness is an expression of compassion and kindness when we think about it.

The new clothes we've been given to wear are the character of Christ.

One commentator writes, *"If you're not wearing compassion and kindness and forgiveness and love,"* (and we could also add humility, patience, gentleness and other Christ-like virtues) " *then you're only half dressed!"*

So, Paul is saying this - life without Christ is meaningless! But life with Christ is transforming! Falsehood is replaced by truth. And the thief becomes a philanthropist. Did you notice that in the reason Paul gives for work? *He who has been stealing must steal no longer, but must work, doing something useful with his own hands, that he may have something to share with those in need.*

The tongue used to destroy people is now used to encourage and strengthen and build people up, hatefulness becomes compassion and kindness and forgiveness, and dedicated followers of worldly fashions become imitators of God himself.

Can you imagine something very important happening in a person's life but nothing changes? A potentially life changing event occurs but everything remains just as it was.

The day a person receives a university degree for example, after several years of study and hard work. Imagine that person receives the degree and then goes home and does nothing at all. It happens but it is not the way it's meant to be.

Or imagine a couple getting married and then each going home to live with their parents (assuming that's where they lived before they were married!) and nothing changes.

Or that first Easter, and Peter goes back to his fishing boat and spends the rest of his life doing what he did before Jesus called him. And all the other disciples returning to whatever they were doing before Jesus interrupted their lives.

If a wedding or graduation or some other

momentous occasion can be life-changing, then the resurrection of Jesus most certainly demands a response and a change. It validates everything the Gospel claims about Christ, and it confirms everything that Christ requires of us.

One thing Christ requires of us is that we wear the clothes he provides.

It is possible to remain untouched by it all, and that's a choice some people make. But Christ – the Risen Christ – comes to us, and challenges us to do what he did - to leave our old clothes behind and accept the new clothes he offers, the new life that is ours in him, the new nature that is capable of living in God's way.

EPHESIANS
5:1-10

Some years ago, a young couple started attending our church back in Weston-super-Mare for a short while. They had no Christian background. In fact, their whole spiritual experience, such as it was, was gained from the occult and New Age movement, and the almost obligatory experimenting with drugs.

This young family – they had a baby- were made very welcome in our church, and several of us helped and supported them as they set up home on one of the estates not too far from the church.

At the same time, it seems, they were also being helped and supported by a couple of young men from the nearby Mormon Church. And in the end the Mormons won!

Why? Well, the couple had the courtesy to come and tell me their decision, and to thank us for all the help we'd given them, and also to assure us that it wasn't personal. They just didn't feel they should have a foot in two camps.

I asked why they had decided in the end to commit themselves to the Mormons, and the answer was simply this. They knew exactly what was expected of them if they became Mormons. The lifestyle was made very clear to them right down to what they should eat and drink, and what they shouldn't eat and drink. So much for those in our churches who say people aren't interested in church because they don't like being told what to do!

Even in our liberal society where (to echo some Old Testament words) *"everyone does what is right in their own eyes"*, there are those who look for some rigid framework in which to practice their faith. They want to be told what's expected of them.

So, this prompts the question: - *what's expected of us as Christians, as followers of Christ?*

The answer to this question is less precise, less detailed, less prescriptive than that offered by Mormons, or Jehovah's Witnesses for that matter, or many other minority groups.

We can never give a simple but detailed answer to the question – *"what's expected of us as Christians"* – not on the basis of one text or passage of scripture. But these words at the beginning of Ephesian 5 at least point us in the right direction.

Be imitators of God, therefore, as dearly loved children, and live a life of love, just as Christ loved us and gave himself up for us as a fragrant offering and sacrifice to God.

Paul says: ***Be imitators of God, <u>therefore</u>.*** That word, "therefore", points us back to what's gone before – i.e. in chapter 4.

Paul has just said - ***Be kind and compassionate, forgiving one another, just as in Christ God forgave you.*** And God's example of kindness and compassion and forgiveness in and through Christ leads Paul to go on to say this in 5:1.

Be imitators of God

What does this mean? The first thing to note is that, when Paul says, "***Be imitators of God***" the word "***Be***" is better translated as "*become*". It means we should become what we are not at present. It means a new direction to our lives.

<u>***Become***</u> ***imitators of God*** means ***become*** more like him, and the verses that follow spell out something of what this means.

First of all and above all else it means ***live a life of love.*** (verse 2)

If we are going to be imitators of God, we need to remember that God's nature is defined by this word "**love**". His defining characteristic is **love**. ***God is Love*** (1 John 4:8)

There are various Greek words describing different

kinds or aspects of love. There is a word meaning physical love, another meaning brotherly/sisterly love, another meaning affection, parental love, kindness, and, of course, there is the distinctive New Testament word found here — *agape*.

What does *agape* mean? I always feel the meaning of the word "*agape*" is best summed up in the word "*commitment*".

The word "*agape*" is found 252 times in the New Testament. 5 times it is used in connection with wrongdoing, in terms of a *commitment* to wrongdoing. 46 times *agape* refers to love for God, *commitment* to God. 130 times *agape* is used for love for one another, *commitment* to our brothers and sisters in Christ. If you have been keeping track, you will have worked out that-71 other uses of the word "*agape*" are unaccounted for!

Love for God and love for one another are about our commitment to God, wanting the very best for God, and wanting the very best for each other. This is what it means to **Live a life of love".** It means "*Live a life controlled by love; love for God and love for one another*".

But what about those other unaccounted-for times "*agape*" is used in the New Testament?

71 times in the New Testament *agape* is used of God's love for us, God's *commitment* to you and me, and to the world in which we live.

Because of his great love for us, God, who is rich in mercy, made us alive with Christ even when we were dead in transgressions--it is by grace you have been saved (Eph 2:4,5)

When the kindness and love of God our Saviour appeared, he saved us, not because of righteous things we had done, but because of his mercy. (Titus 3:4)

This is how God showed his love among us: He sent his one and only Son into the world that we might live through him. This is love: not that we loved God, but that he loved us and sent his Son as an atoning sacrifice for our sins. (1 John 4:9f)

And Paul reminds us that his call to *live a life of love* is perfectly reasonable because we ourselves are loved by God.

Be imitators of God, therefore, <u>as dearly loved children</u>.

One definition of a Christian is *someone who, through faith in Christ, has become a child of God, a dearly loved child.*

We may have had a terrible childhood. We may have experienced very little human love. But Paul is not basing his call on how other people have treated us. He is saying... ***<u>as dearly loved children</u>***... *live a life of love, just as Christ loved us...* and of course he means *as dearly loved children of a loving* *heavenly Father.*

How has God shown love for us? How's this for starters? The beauty of creation, the warmth and glory of sunshine, the freshness of air, the blessing of rain, the provision of food - all kinds of food. human companionship, health and strength, gifts of imagination and artistic skills.

In other words, God has shown his love for us in the basic necessities of life, and so many extra blessings to enrich our lives.

But supremely God has shown his love for us in Jesus - ***God loved the world so much that he gave his only Son, so that whoever believes in him shall not die, but have eternal life....***

God gave himself as the ultimate expression of love.

But it's one thing to say God loves us. It is quite another to know in our hearts that God loves and to receive that love.

Imagine a crisp clear, sunny spring morning. You have a choice. You can keep the doors and windows tightly closed, put a draught stopper at the doors to keep the fresh clean air out, draw the curtains to shut out the sunlight, take any other steps necessary to prevent the light and fresh air getting in.

Or you can throw back the curtains, fling open

the doors and windows and allow the freshness to enter.

It's the same with God's love. We have a choice. We can resist it by allowing ourselves to be ruled by our cold, stubborn hearts and leave God knocking at the door, or we can throw open the door and welcome him in.

Live a life of love means to let God's love into our lives, day by day, and then allow that love to rule us, control us, guide us, govern us in all we do. The result will be that the love we receive will enable us, empower us to love others.

It is very simple. If you are not a child of God, you cannot *live a life of love*, not by God's standard of love.

If we are going to be imitators of God and live a life of love, then we need to remember who we are in Christ. We need to find our identity and security as dearly loved children, and then, and only then, will we have the freedom to live a life characterised by sacrifice, self-denial, generosity, faithfulness, obedience to our heavenly Father's will.

In other words, only then will we be able to show the kind of love seen in Christ, includes loving not only our friends but our enemies too.

And that means that the love Paul is writing about has to be more than sentiment, feelings, and simply being good-natured towards people. It's about commitment to God and his purposes, and commitment to people.

But there is something else we have to do if we are going to *"Be imitators of God".*

v 8   *live as children of light*

What does this mean? There are various ways of understanding this.

(a) we should radiate joy, warmth, love, goodness, truth, or (b) we should live in such a way that we are not afraid to have our thoughts, words and actions exposed to the light, or (c) we should live as those whose life is itself a light to others, guiding them to the feet of the Saviour, or most probably (d) we should live as those whose whole life is created and nurtured, guided and directed by the Light of the World - Jesus Christ.

Or perhaps it means all of these!

If we need any amplification of this, Paul reminds us of those who live in darkness, and the words he uses to describe those who live in darkness are not very attractive.

Or to change the metaphor, if we are thinking about the fragrance of Christ spreading through his people, Paul reminds us of some unpleasant odours.

Sexual immorality, impurity, greed, obscenity,

foolish talk, coarse joking.

In chapter4:22-24 we have more aspects of darkness - lying and deceit, discouraging, destructive criticism, stealing, bad language, bitterness, immorality.

We could add many other "dark" words - violence, hatred and divisions, poverty, death, destruction, pessimism, distrust.

Paul reminds us that such things are inappropriate for Christians.

The call to *live as children of light* is a call to learn the discipline of ordering our lives in such a way that they are pleasing to the Lord.

One more aspect of being *imitators of God.*

Be very careful how you live.

Actually the Greek means "*walk circumspectly*" or "*watch your step!*", otherwise you will stumble and fall.

Have you ever noticed that it is not usually big things we fall over? Sometimes when people fall over, they don't even know what caused them to fall. So we say they tripped over a blade of grass, or a matchstick or something similar.

You don't often hear of people tripping over park benches, or bus shelters, or even council litter bins!

It tends to be the little things that cause us to stumble. We twist our ankle on a twig, or slip on a banana skin, or more likely, a wet leaf. A paving slab only has to project half an inch above the rest, and down we go!

As someone once said: *"Satan never dangles big sins in front of us to tempt us - it's always little things - things that hardly seem to matter".*

Life is full of many little temptations and distractions, things that hardly seem to matter yet they so easily trip us up.

Watch your step! Be careful how you live!

If we deliberately choose to go where we are likely to meet temptation, we are asking for trouble. Every one of us should be aware of those situations where we don't trust ourselves.

But it isn't only about tripping up or falling. It's also about our responsibility towards other Christians. Those who are gardeners know what it's like when you do a bit of weeding in the flower beds or vegetable plot. You have to be careful where you walk - *"walk circumspectly"* - or you may do irreparable damage to the plants you want to keep!

During the school holidays, when I was about 16 or 17, I used to work for the Forestry Commission, and in summer I had to *"walk circumspectly"* for two reasons. The first reason can be summed up in one word – wasps! Perhaps two words – wasps' nests! If I wasn't careful and observant – *circumspect* – I could easily tread on a wasp's nest, which would actually do more harm to me than to the wasps.

But more to the point, the other reason why I had to be careful was that, during summer, we had the strange sounding task of weeding trees.

It isn't perhaps so strange if I tell you the trees in question were tiny oak saplings about 4-6 inches tall, and the problem was that the grass would grow round these saplings, reaching up 12" or more. The grass would then die back, and form a thick thatch and smother the saplings.

So my task was to cut the grass with a sickle or grass hook, but first I had to find the sapling! And if I didn't walk carefully I could tread on it with disastrous results!

"*Walk circumspectly*" because we may do damage to our selves, or to others. In our words, actions, attitudes we can do immense harm to others, whether they are new Christians or mature Christians.

We can do harm by a poor example, or a careless word. In the book of Isaiah we find some verses concerning the servant of God - verses that Christians have always seen fulfilled in Jesus Christ:

He will not shout or cry out, or raise his voice in the streets. A bruised reed he will not break, and a smouldering wick he will not snuff out.

Imitators of God must watch their step so that they don't break a bruised reed or snuff out a smouldering wick.

Be imitators of God. But how can we imitate our mysterious, awesome God who is far beyond our imagination or understanding? God, who is glorious in majesty, mighty, holy and pure.

Jesus said - *whoever has seen me, has seen the Father.* God mercifully and graciously sent Jesus into the world to show us what God is like.

If you want to know what it means to be an imitator of God, and to live a life controlled by love, to live as a child of light, and to be very careful how you live, look at Jesus, follow him, and ask the Holy Spirit to help you day by day to become more like Jesus.

And who knows? Perhaps then the fragrance of Christ will spread throughout this church and the local community.

EPHESIANS 5:15,16

(This sermon can also be found in my book of sermons on "Stewardship" – "A Living Sacrifice")

Ephesians 5:15-16 **"Be very careful, then, how you live—not as unwise but as wise, making the most of every opportunity..."**

Let me ask you a question: *What do you think? Does the church - your church - spend its time wisely or unwisely?*

I'm sure it would be very interesting to hear some of the answers to this question, but I'm not sure such an exercise would be very helpful, because the question is a bit of a trick question in some ways. It's a trick question because whether or not the church spends its time wisely or unwisely depends very much on how you and I spend our time. The fact is that **we** are the church!

Remember the old rhyme?
The church is not a building,
the church is not a steeple,

the church is not a resting place,
the church is - PEOPLE.

The church is made up of people who love Christ, who have given their lives to him, who want to follow Jesus, obeying his commands, trusting him for forgiveness, trusting him with our whole life here and hereafter. **We** are the church, not the church building. And we are the church not only when we meet together for worship, but we are still the church when we are scattered across the community throughout the week.

So, with this in mind, what do you think... *Does the church - your church - spend its time wisely or unwisely?* In other words, how do you and I spend our time? Do we spend our time wisely or unwisely?

In this series of sermons on Stewardship we come now to the **stewardship of time** which may, in turn, touch very briefly on the stewardship of talents, gifts etc. because time is the most precious gift we're given, and we are going to consider how we use this God-given gift.

Our text is there in Ephesians 5:15-16 '**Be very careful, then, how you live—not as unwise but as wise, making the most of every opportunity...**' The only problem is that the text does not have the word 'time' in it, at least not in the NIV translation.

In Ecclesiastes 3 the word 'time' appears over and

over again... **a time to be born and a time to die, a time to plant and a time to uproot, a time to kill and a time to heal etc.**

The Greeks had two words for 'time' – the word *chronos* meaning time measured in hours, minutes, seconds, i.e. duration of time. This is the time we are most conscious of. Indeed, it might be true to say we live in a culture that is ruled by time. We measure it as precisely as we can and then we become slaves to it. New technology is constantly being developed to do things more and more quickly.

The main processor in the computer I use nowadays is hundreds of times faster than the one I was using back in the 1990s, although that doesn't necessarily mean it can do things hundreds of times more quickly. The internet (or rather my means of accessing the internet) is certainly faster than it was when I first used it.

And yet we still don't have time for this, or that, whatever this or that may be! Today's workforce is considerably more stressed than, say, 40 -50 years ago, not necessarily because of greater pressures at work, although this may be a factor, but often the stress is the result of trying to fit too many things into life outside of work.

We seem to be ruled by time, and the result is that we are stressed, irritable, frustrated, impatient, overwhelmed, exhausted and so on, and this isn't at all what God intended for us. It is using time unwisely.

God created time and he didn't create it to make life more stressful, but this is what happens when we allow *chronos* time to rule us.

The other Greek word for time is *Kairos,* and this is quite different. *Kairos* means 'the opportune moment, the right time.

In the Greek translation of the Old Testament, known as the Septuagint, the scholars working on this translation chose this second word, *kairos* to translate the Hebrew word *'eth. Eth* is the word used over and over again in Ecclesiastes 3. There is a *right <u>moment</u> to be born and a right <u>moment</u> to die… a right time to plant and a right time to uproot.*

In our text in Ephesians 5:16 the word 'opportunity' translates *kairos* which means that the word 'time' does appear in the text, but not in our NIV translation. **Make the most of every opportunity, make every moment count**. This is what we mean by the stewardship of time, and if we are going to do this, if we are going to make every moment count, there are some things we need to understand concerning time itself.

For example, it may be stating the obvious, but **time passes!** In fact, I would even venture to suggest that time is the most perishable commodity we know. Time is a wonderful gift from God to each and every one of us, yet it slips through our fingers like sand. Of all the gifts God gives us, time is the only one which he gives sparingly, just one moment at a time, and when that moment has been used, whether for good or ill, it is gone for ever.

A former Baptist Union President, John James, once wrote... *Each day the Bank named 'TIME' opens a new account. It allows no balances, no overdrafts. If we fail to use the day's deposit, the loss is ours.'*

We can never **save** time; we only use it more efficiently and more effectively. We can't carry some forward to the next day. Each day begins with 24 hrs, 86,400 seconds, and by the end of the day every one of those 86,400 seconds will have been used, spent right down to the last one. As each moment passes, that's it - it's gone for ever! This minute I am now living will never be lived again. It will never be repeated and can never be retrieved. It can be wasted but never recycled! But one day it will be **recalled** because we are accountable for the way we use this precious gift called time.

So the first thing we need to come to terms with if we are going to **make the most of every opportunity, make every moment count** is the passing nature of time, the most perishable commodity I know of.

The second thing we need to understand if we are

going to **make every moment count** is *how short a lifetime is* even if we live to be a hundred!

When we are young, with a lifetime ahead of us, it seems as if we have all the time in the world, all the time in the world to make amends, and correct our mistakes, and do something with our lives. We seem to have plenty of time when we're young and sometimes time can't pass quickly enough. But it all looks very different from where I stand now.

A cartoon character was once speaking to a friend, and he said this... *God put me on this earth to accomplish a certain number of things; right now, I'm so far behind I'll never die!'* Don't you believe it! It's been said that if we knew the world was coming to an end in five minutes time, the telephone systems of the world, landlines and mobile systems, would be jammed as people tried to call loved ones to make amends for some silly quarrel or some mistake. We live most of our lives on the assumption we're immortal, and so we live with so many loose ends and unfinished business, and then suddenly we discover that time is beginning to run out.

A clock in Chester Cathedral has the following lines inscribed on it...

When as a child I laughed and wept,
time crept;
When as a youth I dreamt and talked,
time walked;

When I became a full-grown man,
time ran;
When older still I daily grew,
 time flew,
Soon I shall find on travelling on
- time gone!

If this is all a bit depressing, then be assured this is not my intention. Surely the brevity of life should encourage us to **make every moment count, make the most of every opportunity.** Life is very precious. I'm sure we become more and more aware of this with each passing year. And one of the concerns many people have is that at the end of our days, we can look back and say 'I've wasted it; I've wasted all those years', whereas our aim ought to be to echo Paul's words when he says in 2 Tim 4:7 **I have fought the good fight, I have finished the race, I have kept the faith.**

Notice there that when Paul says **I have finished the race'** he doesn't mean he came first! Paul doesn't see life as a competition where we have to come first. I once heard someone say that the aim in this race isn't to beat everyone else; it's simply to finish well.

The third thing we need to understand is this: **we have to live according to God's timescale and not our own.**

I recall some time ago an occasion when a missionary, serving in DR Congo came to speak at a midweek meeting. The meeting was supposed to start at 7.30 p.m., but people had not yet settled down and some were still arriving. I suggested to the missionary that we ought to wait just a little longer, to which the response was that we were working to 'Congo time'. Presumably 'Congo-time' bears little relation to standard time!

A man once rushed on to the platform at a railway station one morning and asked the porter what time the 8.01 train leaves. 'At 8.01' was the obvious answer. 'Well' said the man, 'it's 7.59 by my watch, 7.57 by the town clock and 8.04 by the station clock. Which clock am I to go by?' 'You can go by any clock you like,' said the porter, 'but you can't go by the 8.01 train *because it's already left!'*

We can't live by our own timescale, or any other, for that matter, other than God's timescale because God is the one who determines the right time. He is the one who creates the opportunities, and the important thing to remember is that God has no concept of 'tomorrow'. For God it's always **now**!

So then, ***time passes and cannot be retrieved, life is short, and we can't live by our own timescale***. And with this in mind, Paul urges us to ***be very careful how we live, making the most of every opportunity.***

But how? How do we set about making the most of every opportunity? How do we make every moment count? Paul recognises the difficulty. He recognises the distractions. He knows how easy it is to be diverted. Indeed, this is why he says this: *make the most of every opportunity <u>because the days are evil.</u>*

'the days are evil'... there are many forces at work to distract and lead us astray, and tempt us to fritter away the time so that we waste opportunities. How then are we to 'make every moment count'?

One thing it doesn't mean is that we burn ourselves out in an endless round of activity! This doesn't impress God at all, and it isn't what we mean by making every moment count. In fact, sometimes it's the people running around in circles who are the ones who are wasting time, making a good impression on other people perhaps but actually achieving very little.

What does the writer of Ecclesiastes say? *'There is a time for everything - a right time/right moment for everything'.* a time to be silent as well as a time to speak, time to be doing and a time to be resting, for giving and receiving, serving and being served, using our energy and recharging our batteries, which suggests that conversely there is also a wrong time. The problem is knowing when to be silent, when to speak, knowing the right way to use the time, recognising the opportunities that present themselves to us, and understanding the nature of those opportunities and how to make the most of them.

Paul says here in v 15 - *be very careful how you live*

- not as unwise but as wise. So we need wisdom and discernment if we are going to make every moment count for God, and this wisdom comes from God himself through the Holy Spirit. If God determines the right time, then we need God's wisdom in order to understand how to use our time and how to recognise these opportunities.

This means that one way to use our time is to pray for wisdom regarding our use of the rest of our time. I understand wisdom as being the knowledge of what to do in a given set of circumstances. In other words, doing or saying the right thing at the right time. Wisdom literature in the Old Testament is all about instructing in how to do the right thing at the right time. We need to ask God to give us the gift of wisdom - divine wisdom.

We can, of course, be worldly wise. Worldly wisdom comes with experience, but experience takes time to accumulate, and in making every moment count for God and making good use of every opportunity, we can't always wait for the accumulation of experience, and we can't risk some of the costly mistakes we might so easily make in the process. This is why we need to ask God to help us and give us his gift of wisdom.

In v 17 Paul also reminds us that we need to understand what the Lord's will is - *do not be foolish, but understand what the Lord's will is.*

One of the biggest problems of the Christian life, however, is discerning God's will. 'How do we know what God's will is?' is a question I've often been asked. My suspicion is that part of the problem is that we don't give ourselves sufficiently to prayer and Bible reading. Understanding God's will takes time and effort, but having said this, surely discovering and understanding God's will is time well spent, especially if we also put into practice what we have discovered.

Meanwhile, what can we say about God's will in the context of Ephesians? We can say this - that we have been created to serve. In Ephesians 2:10 we read: *we are God's workmanship, created in Christ Jesus to do good works, which God prepared in advance for us to do.* Some time ago I came across a useful suggestion as to what this means in practice. The writer said that it means that I will endeavour to make Christ look great in every area of my life. In fact, isn't this what Christian stewardship is really all about? Making Christ look great in every area of our lives?

This doesn't mean we have to drop everything that isn't to do with church. It doesn't mean we fill our time with door-to-door evangelism, or preaching at our work colleagues, or turning every conversation round to the gospel. We don't have to give up everyday living to be better stewards of our time and opportunities. The gospels themselves are an edited version of Jesus' life; they don't give us every detail of how he filled his time. In the gospel record we find Jesus preaching, proclaiming God's kingdom and its values, but we also find that he took time to rest, and relax, and we find that he joined in celebrations, enjoyed dinner parties, spent time with friends, built and maintained relationships, and went about doing good. All of this was part of God's work, but it wasn't all preaching and engaging in deep and meaningful spiritual discussions. Jesus' life had its lighter moments too.

There are four important aspects of life that make up a balanced lifestyle, and our lives should include all four. This isn't a list to work down, moving on to the next area if we have time. The aim is to manage our time to include all four. The most important is **our relationship with God**, and this means maintaining our relationship with God on a daily basis, usually through prayer and Bible reading, and sometimes even just making time to be still before God.

And then we have our **family relationships** and responsibilities and obligations, if we have a family or are part of a family. If we don't have a family, then perhaps we substitute our closest friends here.

The third aspect of a balanced life is our **local church**. This is where practical service often comes in, along with building and maintaining relationships, fellowship with our brothers and sisters in Christ, supporting and encouraging and sharing the load. This means we should consider not only what the church can offer us, but also what can we offer to God through the church. And this even includes those who are housebound.

The fourth aspect of a balanced life is our **relationships with those who do not yet know Christ**, perhaps people at work, or our neighbours, or the people we meet in the shops or in the course of our daily lives. This is about how much time we spend getting alongside people beyond the church circle, getting to know them, finding ways, or even learning how, to serve them better.

Returning to the question at the beginning of this chapter: *Does the church - your church - spend its time wisely or unwisely?* How are **you** using this gift of time? Wisely? Or unwisely? According to God's will or determined by your own interests first and foremost? One day every one of us will have to answer for the way we have used this precious gift of time and the opportunities that have come our way.

As a closing thought, here is something Senator Elizabeth Dole once said: *'Life is not just a few years to spend on self-indulgence and career advancement. It is a privilege, a responsibility, and a stewardship to be lived according to a much higher calling.'*

A Prayer:

Forgive us, Lord, when we are rooted to the earth, unable to see beyond the present, and blind to the glory of your presence. We become engrossed in what is happening now, and we forget all that you yet have in store for us. We are so concerned with what is immediate, temporary, and short-lived that we leave ourselves no time for the things that are eternal and full of your love. Lift up our heads, that we may see Christ in all his glory and all things in their true perspective. Lord, through your Holy Spirit working in us, show us day by day how to make Christ look great in all the circumstances and situations of life. For we pray this in His name. Amen

EPHESIANS
5:21-33

According to the writer of Ecclesiastes *there is nothing new under the sun.* For example, the Women's Lib movement can be said to have begun in the 1960s with the likes of Germaine Greer, or even at the end of the 19th century and the beginning of the 20th century with the suffragette movement. But actually it goes back at least 2000 years to the time when Jesus came along and gave honour and respect and dignity to women in a society that, by and large, looked down on women.

Even the apostle Paul himself was not the male chauvinist many imagine him to be; he preached a radical gospel, telling women, and children and slaves, that they too are made in the image of God, that they too are valued and loved by God in Christ, that Christ died for them, and that *There is neither Jew nor Greek, slave nor free, male nor female, for you are all one in Christ Jesus. If you belong to Christ, then you are Abraham's seed, and heirs according to the promise.*

This was a radical message in a society where men ruled, and women were sometimes seen as just possessions.

But such a message, when worked out in practice, was in danger of creating problems as newly liberated women suddenly began to exercise their freedom, and as husbands started reacting in a heavy-handed way to this new wave of teaching that was threatening the social order. Consequently Paul found it necessary to guide these new believers in Ephesus.

Before we charge into what looks like a minefield, let me make some preliminary comments.

(i) we need to take note of the fact that this teaching is for <u>Christian</u> households. The Letter to the Ephesians was written to the believers at Ephesus.

Ephesus was a great city, ranked as one of the greatest cities in the ancient world, and certainly the most important city in Asia Minor. But these instructions were not expected to be adopted in all households in this great city.

These are rules for Christian households, for homes where Jesus Christ is Lord, homes with families whose members are committed to living according to the teachings that Paul has already set out in the first four and a half chapters of this letter to the Ephesians.

(ii) Trinitarian theology has something to say in terms of human relationships and an understanding of what we mean when we talk about equality.

Christian doctrine teaches that there is one God who presents himself to us in three different ways. He is, we might say, a three-dimensional God, with a dimension called the Father, a dimension called the Son, and a dimension called the Holy Spirit.

How do these relate to each other? They are equal in essence, nature, being. We call this *ontological equality*. The Father is not superior to the Son; the Son is not superior to the Holy Spirit. They are equal in their being.

But the three Persons of the Trinity have different functions, different contributions to make, and there's a hierarchy within the Godhead, chain of command. We call this *functional subordination.*

The Son does the will of the Father; he is equal to but also under the authority of the Father.

The Holy Spirit does the will of the Father and the Son; he is equal to but also under the authority of the Father and the Son.

I believe this has some relevance as we look at the passage here in Ephesians 5.

(iii) all that we read in vv 22-33 is Paul developing

the general principle we find in v 21 - *Submit to one another out of reverence for Christ*

You see, none of us is supposed to lord it over other people. As followers of Jesus, how we relate to one another in mutual love and respect is an expression of worship. All believers are called to submit to one another, including both wives and husbands. What Paul is about to do is spell out what this means for each.

What does it mean for the wife to submit to the husband and for the husband to submit to the wife *out of reverence for the Lord?*

Well, for the wife, Paul holds on to the word "*submit*". The problem for us nowadays is that we have a negative view of what this means, because the word "*submit*" is misunderstood and misapplied in the world. It is seen as implying weakness and vulnerability and inferiority and weakness and vulnerability are not prized in the wider world.

What does "*submit*" mean? It doesn't mean slavery. Paul has another word for that. It doesn't mean obey. Paul has another word for that. It doesn't mean domestic bondage, or the surrender of all rights, or inferiority. Nor is Paul encouraging a domestic dictatorship, and that the husband has a divine right to rule the home with a rod of iron.

This command for wives to submit to their

husbands does not mean they become a door mat to be walked over. It does not mean they lose their identity, or that they don't have any input in family discussions and decisions.

Here's how one writer puts it - *genuine Biblical submission is this: A divine calling to honour and affirm the husband's leadership and help him carry it out.*

This is a far cry from the picture painted in today's world where submission is seen as a form of enslavement. And perhaps it is also a far cry from many a modern woman's agenda and understanding of her role in marriage.

You may have heard about the bride-to-be who became more and more nervous as the big day approached.

It wasn't the idea of marriage itself that worried her; it was the actual wedding service, there in the church with everyone looking at her.

On the wedding day she was almost going to pieces with worry, but her mother gave her some advice.

She said "Look, there's only three things you need to focus on. If you focus on these three things, you'll be fine.

The first is walking down the aisle. Just focus on walking down the aisle of the church. I know its rather long, but just concentrate on that. Don't be distracted by those on either side of the aisle. Just focus on getting to the end of the aisle.

Next, focus on the altar. That's where you're aiming, so make your way down the aisle to the altar. There you will stand before God with the man you love and will make vows to God and him. Focus on the altar that represents the love God has for you in Jesus Christ.

And finally, focus on the hymn that we're all going to sing. In poetry and song, the hymn embodies God's love for you in Christ, your love for your husband and his love for you. So focus on the hymn – the music and the words.

So, just focus on those three things and you'll be OK. Walking down the aisle, standing before the altar and listening to the hymn."

The bride was very grateful for this advice. The time came and before she knew it, she and her father were standing at the door of the church. And she set off down the aisle with a look of serenity and calm determination on her face.

As she passed her family and friends, they began to understand why she seemed so relaxed. Along with that look of calm determination, she was mumbling three words over and over to help calm her nerves.

"Aisle, Altar, Hymn." she kept saying quietly to herself. "Aisle, Altar, Hymn. Aisle, Altar, Hymn."

This seems to be a neat summary of the agenda of some brides today! But Paul says *Wives, submit to your husbands as to the Lord.*

To submit means *to set aside one's own will for that of another.* And if this is a problem, perhaps we need to note that Jesus sets us an example throughout his life.

As a child, Jesus submitted to his earthly parents. Can you imagine that? In his letter to the Colossians Paul says Christ is the *image of the invisible God, the firstborn of all creation, by him all things were created.*

Can you imagine that? The Creator setting an example by surrendering his own rights and submitting to the authority of his parents.

As Jesus grew up, he was above all else subject to his heavenly Father's will, including in the Garden of Gethsemane, when Jesus said, "Not my will but yours be done".

And then there was that ultimate act of submission as Jesus allowed himself to be nailed to the cross.

Paul doesn't have this in mind, I don't think, when he gives this instruction to wives, but remember this – The Son of God is equal with the Father - neither inferior nor superior. But he set aside his own will for the will of the Father. That's what submission means - *taking second place.*

Notice this also that Paul says *Wives, submit to your husbands <u>as to the Lord</u>.*

He is saying that there are limits to a wife's devotion to her husband. This command is conditional. The relationship between a husband and wife is determined by another man – Jesus Christ. And the wife is not expected to do anything that is dishonouring or unacceptable to her Lord and Saviour - *"as to the Lord"* is a reminder that the woman's primary relationship is not to her husband but to her Lord and Saviour, Jesus Christ.

When Paul later writes *as the church submits to Christ, so also wives should submit to their husbands in everything* "everything" does not include anything immoral or inappropriate for a disciple of Christ. It does not include anything covered in the earlier teaching in chapter 4, for example.

"Everything" is placed in the context of a Christian marriage where both husband and wife are committed to learning to be *imitators of God and living a life of love and avoiding every kind of immorality – living as children of light.*

Wives, submit to your husbands as to the Lord.

Imagine you own a priceless Ming dynasty vase, and you hand it over to someone for them to keep it safe. That would require a lot of faith, trust, respect for the person, believing that they will not harm it. What Paul is asking Christian wives to do here requires respect and faith and trust and belief in the husband. He is asking wives to let their husbands be the leader in their family.

He is asking them to trust the husband not to make any decision without thinking of what's best for his wife and family, not to make any decision or do anything without first talking it over and agreeing together, trusting the husband won't be selfish and won't use his authority to exploit or hurt or abuse her. And this requires respect and faith and trust.

But, of course, all this is only half the story.

v 25 - *Husbands, love your wives, just as Christ loved the church and gave himself up for her*

Husbands, love your wives – I don't imagine we would have any problem with this. But read on. Are there any limits to this love? By what standard are we to measure this love? *Husbands, love your wives just as Christ loved the church and gave himself up for her.*

The standard by which we measure this love is no less than the standard of Christ's love for us. The reference point for the wife's duty to her husband is Jesus Christ, and he places limits on how far the wife goes in her submission to her husband.

The reference point for the husband is also Jesus Christ, but this time there seem to be no limits as to how far the husband should go in demonstrating his love for his wife - ***as Christ loved the church <u>and gave himself up for her.</u>***

Jesus Christ set no limits to his love for us. Not even death and all the pain and suffering and humiliation of crucifixion - not even this was enough to set limits to his love for you and me.

Husbands, love your wives with the limitless love of Christ as your standard.

This means not lording it over the wife but serving, as Christ served the church, putting her welfare above everything else. The picture is that of leadership through loving and sacrificial care. It's a picture of servant leadership, as modelled by the *servant king.*

Now, I said earlier that to submit is to take second place. What do we have here regarding the husband's duty to his wife? Isn't this kind of love also about taking second place? Isn't it about setting aside one's own interests for the sake of the other partner.

This is the kind of love Paul has in mind. Limitless, selfless love seen in Jesus. The kind of love that puts self in second place.

I don't know if this is a true story, although the main character's name must be real because you wouldn't make up a name like "Johnny Lingo".

Johnny was a handsome bachelor in a village where the custom was that a man would pay a dowry to the father in order to be granted permission to marry the daughter.

The average dowry price for a bride was three cows, although an exceptionally beautiful girl might go for as high as five cows.

One day, Johnny Lingo went to the father of a girl called Sarita to negotiate a dowry. Tongues in the village soon began to wag, especially as it was well known that Sarita was not very pretty. In fact, she was thought to be rather on the plain side.

On the other hand, Johnny was well known for being able to drive a hard bargain so the word was he might be able to get permission in Sarita's case for as low as just one cow.

*Johnny Lingo did nothing of the sort. He marched up to Sarita's father and offered **eight** cows for her hand in marriage.*

Eight cows! It was unheard of! No one had ever paid such a high price for a bride. And certainly not for such a plain woman as Sarita!

But after the wedding, a strange thing happened.

Sarita's head was held high. Her eyes sparkled. It's said that she beamed with an inner glow. And in the years that followed, she became known as the most beautiful woman in the entire village. People would travel many miles to see her. Her beauty was almost legendary.

One day, Johnny was asked why he had paid such a high price for a wife. He replied, "I really loved Sarita and wanted to express the high value of our marriage. Her self-esteem has been raised through realising that her dowry price was higher than any other woman in the village."

Then with a grin, he added, "But the other reason I had was that I wanted to marry an eight-cow wife."

Sarita changed because of the love and the worth, the high value the husband gave to the marriage.

God has paid the highest possible price for you and me because he loves us. He didn't pay for us in cows, but something far better - in the life and death of His one and only Son. And this makes everyone of us priceless.

The command to husbands is love their wives in the same way - *just as Christ loved the church and gave himself up for her.*

Wives, submit to your husbands as to the Lord. Husbands, love your wives just as Christ loved the church and gave himself up for her.

It's often said that it takes two to make a good marriage, and what that means is that both husband and wife have to work at it. But Paul is saying, *Actually, it takes three to make a really good marriage!*

You see, even two atheists could have a good marriage, but Paul is saying - *it is better if there are three, as long as the third partner in a marriage is Jesus!*

When Jesus Christ is the head of the Christian home, and when he is allowed to reign, and when his word is taken seriously, then we have the potential for marriage and family life as God intends it.

Paul gives us the general principle – ***Submit to one another out of reverence for Christ.***

In all life's settings, we have the opportunity to tell, to show, to demonstrate to our families and friends and wider community, the difference Christ makes as he works in our hearts and lives and relationships, working to offer an alternative lifestyle, a better way of living and relating to other people.

EPHESIANS 6:10-20

Do you know what I believe is the Devil's worst nightmare? I believe it is Christian believers taking seriously and applying Paul's instructions here in his letter to the Ephesians, especially the instructions based on the general principle stated back in 5:21 - *Submit to one another out of reverence for Christ.*

In previous passages Paul has applied this general principle in various contexts. Marriage, for example, as well as the family (children & parents), and the workplace.

The Devil's worst nightmare is people living according to God's Word as spoken through his servant Paul, and so we find that the Devil will attack us especially at these points - - in our marriages, in our families and in the workplace.

He will do all he can to disrupt us, to tempt us, to distract us & make it difficult to be imitators of God, living a life of love, living as children of light, in these relationships and places.

It's in these situations that we will find ourselves engaged *in spiritual warfare.* But I wonder what comes to mind when we hear those words: "spiritual warfare"?

For some, the phrase conjures up images seen in a science fiction film with grotesque demons fighting beautiful angels, and our task is simply to support the angels with prayer.

Other people go to the opposite extreme and refuse to accept that there is such a thing as spiritual warfare.

The New Testament is quite clear that there is a battle taking place, but it isn't so much about great cosmic battles. More often than not it's fought in the hearts and minds and lives of people, especially believers, as we face temptation and failure and as we take up the challenge to evangelise and witness for Christ.

Paul has already been hinting at ways in which the Devil can attack us in the verses leading up to our passage, where he focusses on submitting to one another. The Devil will attack us especially at these points, in our marriages, in our family life, and in the workplace because human nature can be such that the idea of submitting to another person is not at all appealing.

The Devil will do all he can to disrupt us, to

tempt us, to distract us and make it difficult to be imitators of God, living a life of love, living as children of light in these relationships and places.

It's in these situations (and others) where we may well find ourselves engaged *in spiritual warfare.*

Paul was aware of all this and so he urges the Church, by which I mean the community of believers gathered together, meeting and working and serving together - he urges them to take certain steps to protect themselves from the Devil's schemes and spiritual powers and forces.

Paul's words here apply to each individual member of the church, the building blocks of the church, and this is how we tend to understand and apply this passage. But we need to appreciate also that Paul was writing to the church at Ephesus as a whole.

This letter will have been read out to the church gathered together, perhaps in the context of worship. In Baptist terms, this might mean something akin to reading it out at a church meeting. These verses apply to the life of the local church as a body.

Spiritual warfare then is, I believe, what Paul has in mind in these verses here in Ephesians 6:10-20. Here in this passage we have a reminder of the **enemy** we face, our **main tactic** for fighting this war, and the **weapons** we have available.

First, **the enemy.**

Verses vv 11 and 12 - *Put on the full armour of God so that you can take your stand against the devil's schemes. For our struggle is not against flesh and blood but against the rulers, against the authorities, against the powers of this dark world and against the spiritual forces of evil in the heavenly realms.*

These verses tell us some important things about the enemy.

1 The Devil is real.

This is not a common or popular view these days, even among Christians, but the Bible seems to be crystal clear about this, that there is such a spiritual being as the Devil, Satan. Otherwise, Paul would have no need to write these verses here in Ephesians.

If we don't believe the Devil is real, then straightaway we've given him the advantage in this struggle, because one of his strategies is to persuade us that he doesn't exist!

2 Our enemy is powerful.

Remember what Paul says. *Our struggle is not against flesh and blood.*

Humans are responsible for a great deal of evil in the world, but ultimately, says Paul, the real enemy is not *flesh and blood* but something much greater, more powerful, more sinister, more dangerous.

2000 years later we face the same enemy. We may see evil surfacing in the materialism of our age, or the curtailing of religious freedom, or in crime and poverty and injustice, in racism, in drug abuse and in many other ways, and humans are responsible and accountable for being agents of evil, but the real enemy is found in what's referred to as the "heavenly realms", or the spiritual realms.

The real enemy works in the background causing all this disruption to society, the real enemy being the Devil.

And he is powerful. Make no mistake. This is what all these words are about - *rulers, authorities, powers, spiritual forces.* This is the language of power, supernatural power. But we shouldn't let such language overwhelm us or frighten us because, although this power is real, God's power is far greater.

The Devil's power has been overcome decisively by Christ's death on the cross, and it will be destroyed completely when Jesus returns.

Nevertheless, we need to understand that all this doesn't stop the devil from trying! And he is still very powerful.

3   Not only this, but **the enemy is also evil.**

If the world has anything to say about the Devil, he is usually depicted as a comical and loveable rogue! He is regarded as just a bit naughty and mischievous, but harmless! I imagine the Devil loves that!

The Bible says this is utter nonsense. The Devil has only one aim and that is to spread evil in the world in general, in the church and in the lives of believers in particular.

He is evil. I always find it useful to remember that the word "evil" is an anagram of "vile" and also "live" backwards, the wrong way round. We might say "evil" is "anti- life". The Devil is absolutely committed to spoiling life, trying to make us live in opposition to God, with no regard for God's will in our lives. He is truly **evil**!

4 The Devil is **crafty, cunning, devious**.

Verse 11 refers to the Devil's *schemes.* Jesus spoke in similar terms when he referred to the Devil as being a wolf in sheep's clothing.

I have already referred to one of the Devil's greatest successes in the modern world – persuading us that he doesn't exist. This is one of his schemes, strategies.

Another strategy is to distract people with a fascination for the supernatural. I've had more than one conversation with people whose exploration of Christianity and the Bible has been limited to studying angels and other peripheral parts of scripture.

Today there seems to be a lot of interest in spirits, as seen in TV programmes like Most Haunted where the presenters try to get in touch with the realm of spirits. *(This sermon was preached in 2009)*. I am sure it is all quite fascinating, but the real danger is that this interest in the supernatural gets mixed with a sort of religious dimension and language, whereas in truth it is all part of the Devil's schemes to distract people from the true gospel.

This then is the **enemy** in this spiritual warfare.

What about our main **tactic** in this spiritual battle?

We find it in v 10 - ***be strong in the Lord and in his mighty power.***

You see, there are two basic mistakes we can make as Christians. One is to be spiritually lazy, and the other is not to trust the Lord. I expect there are other mistakes and dangers too.

Being spiritually lazy means just sitting back and hoping the battle won't touch us. It means letting God get on with being God with no help or interference from us. After all, if there's a spiritual battle going on, then it doesn't really concern me – that's God's concern not mine.

To the spiritually lazy, Paul says – **Be strong, stand up and fight!**

Not trusting in the Lord means we run around in circles, trying to do it all in our own strength, and to such people Paul says - *it's great that you're doing all that fighting but don't rely on yourself –* **trust in the Lord and in his mighty power.** *Rely on God's strength above your own!*

The Christian life is always meant to be a combination of God's strength and our co-operation, and not the other way round - our strength with God's co-operation! That's why I wince when I hear Carey's well-known words quoted the wrong way round: He said, *"Expect great things from God: attempt great things for God"* and **not** *"Attempt great things for God; expect great things from him"*. The latter sounds like us setting the agenda and then asking God to bless it.

Be strong in the Lord and in his mighty power...

There will be times when it's a struggle and we feel like we're losing the battle, and the enemy's power is too much for us. But the tactic is to keep going and don't give up, because our strength is found in God's mighty power and not our own.

Stand firm. Our part in the battle is about holding a position, knowing where we stand and standing firm.

I am reminded of the old hymn that says *On Christ the solid rock I stand; all other ground is sinking sand.*

Stand firm on Christ, the solid rock. In military terms this means occupying the high ground and defending it.

Paul has already described this high ground back in chapters 1 and 2 –
In 1:20 he speaks about God raising Christ *from the dead, seating him at his right hand in the heavenly realms, far above all rule and authority, power and dominion, and every title that can be given, not only in the present age but also in the one to come*.

and in 2:6 - *God raised <u>us</u> up with Christ and seated us with him in the heavenly realms in Christ Jesus,*

That's the high ground we occupy - *seated with Christ in the heavenly realms.*

At last, we come to the **equipment** we have available.

vv 13-18 - *Therefore put on the full armour of God, so that when the day of evil comes, you may be able to stand your ground, and after you have done everything, to stand. Stand firm then, with the belt of truth buckled round your waist, with the breastplate of righteousness in place and with your feet fitted with the readiness that comes from the gospel of peace. In addition to all this, take up the shield of faith, with which you can extinguish all the flaming arrows of the evil one. Take the helmet of salvation and the sword of the spirit, which is the word of God. And pray in the Spirit on all occasions with all kinds of prayers and requests.*

Notice first of all, that Paul says **put on the full armour of God.** It won't do to put on a little piece here and a little piece there - **put on the _full_ armour of God.**

A couple or so years ago – when Christine and I were in France for a few days – we went to Agincourt and visited the visitor centre there. On reflection, this is actually very gracious of the French – providing a visitor centre – considering that an English army numbering at most about 6000 defeated a French army of something like four or five times that many!

In this visitor centre there many interesting displays, including several examples of the armour used back in the 15th century. The armour was heavy requiring heavy horses capable of carrying the fully-clad rider and his weapons.

A Roman soldier's armour, by contrast, was lightweight, practical and developed by the experience gained in thousands of battles. It was mainly defensive armour designed not so much to keep the soldier from dying, but to keep him alive so that he could carry on fighting for the emperor.

Our armour has the same purpose - not so much to keep us from dying but to keep us alive, alive in Christ, alive to go on loving and hoping and serving and witnessing.

Can you see the difference in emphasis there? Keeping the soldier from dying is all about the soldier's well-being, all about the individual. Keeping him alive is about the big picture, and the importance of the battle itself.

There are two main groups of weapons and armour here in Ephesians 6.

The first group is found in vv 14-15, and here we find what might be called the "given" things about being a Christian - truth, righteousness and the readiness to share the gospel. These are given to us when we believe. There's nothing we have to do to get them or use them. The verbs here are in the past tense and are all passive.

the belt of <u>truth</u> buckled around your waist,
the breastplate of <u>righteousness</u> in place,
and your feet fitted with the readiness that comes
from the <u>gospel of peace</u>.

The belt of truth

Truth is vital to our Christian faith because the truth revealed by Jesus sets us free.

The **truth** that, as it were, holds us together is the truth, for example, that God loves us and sent his Son into the world to live and die for our sakes. It is the **truth** that, on the third day he rose from the dead.

The **truth** we uphold and live by is the truth that there are such things as right and wrong and good and evil. There are moral absolutes determined not by what <u>we</u> deem to be right and wrong, but determined by a holy and pure God who wants only the very best for us.

And there is the **truth** that if we choose to ignore God and please ourselves, we are destined to enter a Godless eternity.

The breastplate of righteousness

Righteousness is a word used to describe being right with God through Jesus' death on the cross.

Feet fitted with the readiness that comes from the gospel of peace.

Readiness to share the Gospel is a sign that we have been converted and received Christ as Lord and Saviour. We are given a desire to share the good news of God's grace and mercy with others.

The gospel of peace is peace **with** God, because of God's grace and mercy. It means enjoying fellowship with God, having been reconciled to God through Christ. And it is also the peace **of** God in our hearts.

In Phil 4:7 we read of *the peace of God, which transcends all understanding, will guard your hearts and your minds in Christ Jesus.*

Both of these aspects of peace are worth sharing with others, as opportunities present themselves.

"Readiness" speaks of being prepared to share this good news.

1 Peter 3:15 - *Always be prepared to give an answer to everyone who asks you to give the reason for the hope that you have. But do this with gentleness and respect.*

In verses 16-18 we find the second group of equipment.

The shield of faith – this refers to an active trust in Jesus on a daily basis, believing and trusting in the promises of God and relying on God's power especially in difficult times.

Faith means a real, genuine belief and trust in God as our creator and saviour, a faith that trusts in the presence of God and the power of God and the promises of God.

It may be worth making a brief mention here concerning the shield itself.

Roman soldiers under attack would often stand behind their shields, standing side by side forming a long protective barrier against the enemy's arrows.

Arrows were often soaked in pitch and then the tips set on fire , which explains the reference to flaming arrows here.

The shields were coated in leather which would be soaked in water, and so we have *the shield of faith, with which you can extinguish all the flaming arrows of the evil one.*

We extinguish these flaming arrows with **faith**, believing and trusting in the promises of God and relying on God's power, especially in difficult times.

The helmet of salvation means remembering the sure and certain hope we have in Christ, the assurance that we're saved from the penalty of sin and ultimately from the power and presence of the Devil, an assurance with which to resist any attack, any temptation to doubt our status as children of God.

The sword of the Spirit, which is the word of God Obviously this is what we now know as the Bible which is able to teach us the truth about ourselves, and about God and his will for us.

The Word of God can help us in times of temptation, as it did when Jesus faced the Temptations during his 40 days in the wilderness at the beginning of his earthly ministry. God's Word of truth and light have the power to oppose the Devil's weapons of darkness and ignorance and deceit.

We need to be familiar with the Word of God, and

we need to know how it works and how to use it.

And **Prayer,** especially for other Christians, referred to here as the saints. Prayer also for the proclamation of the gospel – v 19 - *Pray also for me, that whenever I open my mouth, words may be given me so that I will fearlessly make known the mystery of the gospel,*
for which I am an ambassador in chains. Pray that I may declare it fearlessly, as I should.

This really does cover just about everything. If there's a need - pray! If there's a worry or concern - pray! Pray for opportunities to witness. Pray for guidance and strength and wisdom. Pray for ourselves and for one another and for strangers whom we may never meet, but who also need God's power in the face of suffering and persecution and temptation.

There are all kinds of prayer, public, private, and secret; social and solitary; set prayers and sudden prayers: confession of sin, prayers for mercy, and thanksgiving for blessings received.

Prayer is a great and powerful weapon that we sometimes underuse by focussing on small things. At a previous church I tried so hard (but failed) to move our prayer meetings on from praying for Aunt Edie's bunion to much bigger issues. I exaggerate, and it's right to pray for one another, but our prayers shouldn't get stuck at level.

I once heard prayer described as being "subversive", and it can be. Do you realise that by prayer we can gain access even to cabinet meetings and to the heart of government? And in the name of Jesus we can begin to influence decisions.

Sometimes we underestimate the importance of prayer. Sometimes we think of praying as next to doing nothing and we say, "*But it's the least I can do.*"

The **least** we can do? Is that how we view prayer? If there really is a God in heaven who cares and who hears and responds to prayer, then surely prayer is the most we can do!

Prayer does not excuse us from doing what we're capable of doing ourselves, but at same time, through prayer, we call on God who is able to do things we could never do in a million years.

One commentator says this of prayer: *God expects us to pray just as a general expects to hear from his soldiers in the battle.*

Another writer says that '*prayer is a walkie-talkie for warfare, not a domestic intercom for increasing our conveniences*'.

So, we have this armour. Not fancy, ornate armour inscribed with emblems and fancy metal work, but God's armour with its life-giving, life-sustaining protection - truth, righteousness, a readiness to share the gospel, faith in Jesus, hope for the future, the Bible and prayer. These are all the armour and weapons we need for this spiritual warfare, all aimed at enabling us to overcome temptation and discouragement and doubts.

The enemy is real and powerful and evil and scheming. Our main tactic is not to rely on our own strength but to be strong in the Lord and in his mighty power, and our weapons are all about being a Christian and living as a Christian day by day.

Just as we're meant to clothe ourselves daily with the character of Christ, we are also meant to put on this armour each day. It's been provided for us, but we are responsible for wearing it.

The question for us to ask ourselves is this: *Which part of the armour would I never dream of omitting? And which part of the armour do I tend to neglect?*

In other words, do I go into each day properly equipped and protected by the **full armour of God** together with all the resources God makes available for this spiritual warfare?

Put on the full armour of God so that you can take your stand against the Devil's schemes.

EPHESIANS 6:18B

(This was my suggested Text for 2003. It covers a little of the ground already covered but has some newer material too.)

Be alert and keep on praying for all the saints.

I believe God's challenge to us for 2003 and beyond is to make prayer our Number One Priority. I suspect few people would argue with the matter of prayer being very important. With our lips, at least, we affirm the importance of prayer, in theory, even if our practice may not quite match up to the theory. I know mine doesn't, sadly!

In this text, Paul is also saying that prayer is of the utmost importance. He says *always keep on praying for all the saints...*

What he means is, *whatever else you may choose to do, or choose not to do,* *always keep on praying.* Make prayer your Number One Priority.

Prayer is important for at least two reasons:

First, prayer is the means by which we maintain our relationship with God, through constant communication. And our relationship with God is surely the most important thing in our lives.

As we noted in the previous chapter, we are engaged in spiritual warfare, not just now and then but constantly. When we accept Christ as our Lord and Saviour, Satan declares all out war on us. And any soldier will tell you how vital communications are in any battle.

We need to stay in touch with HQ, otherwise we become isolated and helpless, weak and vulnerable. We have to fend for ourselves, and rely on our own resources, which are usually less than adequate for the fight.

Prayer is important because it is the means of staying in contact with God, our commander-in-chief.

The second reason why prayer so important is this. As E M Bounds puts it: ***Prayer is the great universal force to advance God's cause.***

We may not understand how prayer works, and why God chooses this way, but the fact remains that prayer is the means by which we channel God's power. And we certainly need God's power and presence in our lives, and in the life of the church.

We need God's power for the good of our local community. We need God's power to be at work in our nation, and throughout the world.

God is, of course, the sovereign Lord and can work in many ways and in any way he chooses. But he has chosen prayer to be one of the ways through which he works. It is one of the weapons he has given us for use in this spiritual battle.

And it works!

Some time ago, British soldiers were serving in one of the trouble spots somewhere in the world – it may have been Afghanistan - and reports were received that they were complaining that their equipment was outdated and ineffective. Their weapons and other equipment did not work properly.

God does not equip his soldiers with outdated and ineffective weapons and equipment! Prayer works!

But we need to understand this. Before we switch into pantomime mode and say, *"Oh no it doesn't!"*, some prayers will never be answered.

If I sit there at a football match, all despondent and praying that somehow we'll win, do you think God's going to answer that prayer? Probably not. After all, someone supporting the opposing team might well be praying the same prayer on behalf of their team!

This doesn't mean prayer does not work. Prayer will often change circumstances and situations (not football matches, but other more important matters). Amazing things do happen as a result of prayer, but sometimes it isn't the circumstances or situation that needs to be changed. Sometimes it's the people we are praying for who need to be changed, whether it's ourselves or someone on the other side of the world.

We need to be changed sometimes. The people we pray for need to be changed sometimes, so that we and they are able to accept their circumstances or be given grace and strength to deal with the situation.

I read recently of a little girl whose friend, I think it was, was suffering from alopecia – hair loss. The little girl prayed for her friend, but her friend, Amy, continued to lose her hair.

The little girl went on praying the same prayer day after day, week after week, and then one day she changed her prayer - *Dear Jesus – if you won't hold Amy's hair on her head, would you please hold Amy?*

What she had grasped, perhaps without even realising it, was that sometimes God doesn't move mountains – sometimes he moves us.

Prayer works, but sometimes it may work by changing us rather than things and people around us.

That was the experience of the psalmist so often. He starts out in a terrible frame of mind, discouraged, depressed, overwhelmed by his circumstances. But during the course of his prayer, his circumstances do not change but the psalmist's attitude does.

Prayer then is of vital importance. It is important because it maintains our contact with God, and because it is an effective channel of God's power.

But, if prayer is so important, why is it such a struggle? I'm sure a good number of people would agree that prayer is not easy, or is it just me?

Why is it that when we want to pray and read God's word, we are so easily distracted by things outside of us e.g. the front door or telephone, or by our own thoughts and concerns?

If it is so important, why is prayer such a struggle?

I'll tell you. We must not blame everything on Satan as if we ourselves bear no responsibility, but one thing Satan hates more than anything else is a praying Christian.

Satan trembles when he sees
The weakest saint upon his knees!

Do you realise that, when we turn to God in prayer, an alarm sounds in Satan's battle HQ? And he scrambles his forces, and will do just about anything to keep us from praying, including prompting some innocent, well-meaning person to phone us!

So, as soon as we turn to God in prayer, we come under attack and need this armour.

If you need proof of the importance and effectiveness of prayer, then ask yourself why prayer bothers Satan so much.

Be strong in the Lord and in his mighty power says Paul (v 10)
Put on the full armour of God so that you can take your stand against the devil's schemes...

Do you realise that this is the first thing we need to do before we pray. It is when we pray that we are most in need of God's protection, strength, power and help. So Paul says *Put on the full armour of God.* and put it on before you start praying.

It has been said that praying without the armour is like -
Going golfing without taking your golf clubs
Going fishing without your fishing rod
Going shopping without any cash, cheque book or credit cards.

In other words, to be blunt, it is foolish!

Put on the full armour of God
and then *keep on praying for all the saints.*

Keep on praying... This means be devoted to praying for all the saints, commit yourself to praying for all the saints.

"Saints" is, of course, an expression meaning all God's people. Keep on praying for your fellow Christians in your local church, but don't stop there.

Paul says *all the saints* - in other local churches, in other parts of the country, and throughout the world.

Paul also says... *Be alert.*

He is staying with the military images here, and saying *You're on sentry duty, and your role is very important. Don't underestimate it.*

There may be times when others depend on you being their eyes and ears, guarding them against attack. Of course, you can't keep watch over absolutely everyone , so limit yourself so that you can pray specifically and meaningfully for particular situations.

For example, it isn't very easy to be informed and to pray in any meaningful way for the whole work of BMS, but we can focus on one area, country and the missionaries working there.

That's what it means to be alert – being informed.

In our local area, for example, we could pray in particular for, say, a couple of local churches. Perhaps get hold of their church magazine so that you can be informed.

In the local church, there are often a lot of activities and people needing prayer. But don't try and include everything in your prayers; just focus on one or two.

Adopt a Deacon, or a member of the leadership team. And pray also for a number of members, or work through the church membership roll.

It's all to do with being alert, informed and specific in our prayers.

But **what** should we be praying for, whether praying for people we know and see often, or people we may never meet?

Well, what does Paul pray for? What does he ask for in verses 19-20? He's a prisoner at the time of writing, so does he ask to be released? No! Does he ask to be made more comfortable? No!

Pray also for me, that whenever I speak, words may be given me so that I will fearlessly make known the mystery of the gospel, for which I am an ambassador in chains. Pray that I may declare it fearlessly, as I should.
Paul asks them to pray that he may be able to fulfil his commission and be effective in making known *the mystery of the gospel.*

What do you ask for if you ask someone to pray for you? If you were ill, infirm or in some other kind of distress, what would you want people to pray on your behalf?

In the light of Paul's example, what should you be asking for?

We should be asking for this - that even in midst of affliction, God will give us the power and strength to remain faithful and to go on serving him, bearing witness to his loving presence in our lives, and the hope we have in him through Christ.

Be alert and always keep on praying for all the saints.

The challenge of this verse is for us to make prayer our number one priority during 2003 (and beyond!)

If we were going for a fortnight's holiday, not many of us would wake up one day and go, with nothing ready, and, if we are working, not even having booked time off. We make plans for holidays – those of us who are fortunate enough to be able to go away on holiday. If we didn't then the likelihood is that it wouldn't happen, and we would stay at home and watch TV.

It's the same with our prayers. We can pray to God at any time, and we should, but it is also helpful to have a plan, a routine, a prayer time as part of our daily routine. Otherwise it won't happen.

I am sure there are certain things we wouldn't dream of omitting before we leave the house –

washing, and brushing our teeth, combing our hair, getting dressed even! Having breakfast, or a drink at least. Prayer should be included in these essential activities before we even dare to step out of the front door.

> *Be alert and always keep on praying*
> *for all the saints.*

Printed in Great Britain
by Amazon

37110088R00109